SpringerBriefs in Criminology

Translational Criminology

More information about this series at http://www.springer.com/series/10159

Elizabeth A. Stanko • Paul Dawson

Police Use of Research Evidence

Recommendations for Improvement

Springer

Elizabeth A. Stanko
Twickenham, UK

Paul Dawson
London, UK

Additonal material to this book can be downloaded from http://extras.springer.com

ISSN 2192-8533 ISSN 2192-8541 (electronic)
SpringerBriefs in Criminology
ISBN 978-3-319-20647-9 ISBN 978-3-319-20648-6 (eBook)
DOI 10.1007/978-3-319-20648-6

Library of Congress Control Number: 2015945949

Springer Cham Heidelberg New York Dordrecht London

Printed on acid-free paper

Springer International Publishing AG Switzerland is part of Springer Science+Business Media (www.springer.com)

Foreword

If you want to reform your police force from within, this monograph offers you a roadmap to navigate what was once described in a Lords debate on policing in the UK, 'as crawling over broken glass in the dark'. If you are outside and want real reform of front-line operations as opposed to rebadging or superficial gestures it would be wise to take account of Professor Stanko's 10-year and Paul Dawson's 5-year experience on the inside of the London Met attempting evidenced change. It is timely seeking to catch the current tide on evidence-based reform. However reform is not just testing in the UK, as Wes Skogan reminds us from the USA:

> .(It). is hard, the political risks involved are considerable, and efforts to change the police often fall short or fail.[1]

Reformers within the Metropolitan Police have suffered, from my own experience from an almost irrational optimism about their ability to change things. In part at least because they made assumptions about their ability to direct planning in the eighties, to nudge cultural change (the Plus Programme of the early 1990s), to embed diversity sustainably after the Lawrence Inquiry, or transform services dealing with vulnerability in the noughties. The message from the authors is that enthusiasm needs to be leavened with a systematic approach to evidence-based policing (EBP) and follow through on implementation.

Stanko and Dawson's observations are all the more credible because they acknowledge that not everything they attempted or supported worked. Truly reforming policing operations requires resilience as they show, with a telling example of an evidenced reduction of crime in places, that took 8 years, and is still not embedded …

Reform has proved to be a daunting process even for the most powerful, hard-nosed external reformers, who have tended to concentrate over the last 20+ years on developing control mechanisms and structures (see UK Government White Papers of 1993, 2001, and 2010). And an overwhelmingly 'outside-in' approach to reform has not altered the reactive approach of much police work. With some exceptions

[1] G. Skogan, (2008) 'Why reforms fail' Policing & Society. Vol 18, No 1, March, 23–34.

those who have attempted reform from within have also hit big barriers. Even where inroads have been made on corruption, intelligence-led and neighbourhood policing they have slipped over time. The bulk have only made small inroads on police reliance on the 3Rs: response, reactive investigations and random patrol.

Stanko and Dawson describe faltering steps to implement EBP in everyday police operations. They believe that 'to change police practice and behaviour, we must understand it'. p14. On this they are so right. EBP offers an alternative approach to break out of reactivity to what has just happened, by testing what works in stopping what is happening, as opposed to reliance on craft and intuition.

I am a fan of work of this nature, because contrary to the view promoted by some observers I have met genuine reformers from constable to Commissioner, in the Met who have sought to reform planning, corruption, race relations, neighbourhood policing, public order policing and much more. Like these authors, they have run into formidable barriers but to be fair too, there was no guidebook to help them then.

Beyond London others are attempting to follow in their footsteps. This monograph is intended to provide a guide based on the author's experience of 'how' to anticipate and overcome barriers.

The first part of the monograph sensibly encourages the would-be reformer to consider where their organisation sits on the spectrum of evidence-based approach. Positioning oneself and the organisation on EBP is essential for would-be reformers, to determine the degree of support they can expect. As the authors astutely suggest acknowledgement or generic level of senior support is not the same as '*corporate commitment to embed the systematic use of or encourage the generation of evidence within the police organisation*'. p62.

Apparently that commitment didn't exist during the period reviewed. The authors identify a five-step programme of questions to enable reformers to 'situate' themselves. This may seem obvious but I have encountered postgraduate police students at upper mid-level posts and chief officers who had failed to anticipate the power dynamics in their organisations, mistaking a gentle acquiescence from an Assistant Chief Constable or a Chief for approval and vigorous support, which didn't materialise.

Their second is a plea to treat implementation seriously in its own right. This has been the Achilles heel of well-intentioned reform in what reviewers have called human services (education, health and criminal justice).[2] Having interviewed reformers inside and outside policing over the last 20 years, I cannot agree strongly enough on this. The case studies, particularly that of the £11m Diamond Initiative, paint a vivid picture of a worthwhile intervention that just didn't have enough time, or focus on implementation, to fully test its worth. The case studies underline what the authors have written about implementation elsewhere—it needs to be planned and allowed for in the rigours of everyday policing, often neither consideration is allowed for.

The third section is strategic, looking at the challenge of making EBP an organisational approach, rather than occasional foray by devoted individuals.

---

[2] Fixsen, D. et al (2005) *Implementation Research: A synthesis of the literature* Tampa: University of South Florida Press.

This is a very big challenge for all who want to 'Guard my People' as commended on the Queens Police Medal. It is especially so in the face of the squeeze associated with austerity and rising expectations. Examples are offered of success in public confidence, and candidly admitted resistance, so far, in adopting systematic communications to nudge offenders, despite the assistance of the Government Behavioural Insight team. They suggest that learning and focus are pivotal in establishing EBP. Yet their own work reveals a lamentable dearth of training on police science, and little time during crowded working days to redress the gap or catch up with emerging ideas.

On focus, their conclusion from their time in the Met is clear; 'We believe if the delivery of policing is to change, it has to come from the centre of the organisation and be supported by strategic vision—not an agitation from the periphery. Neither individual police officers, nor charismatic academics bring about the necessary foundations for evidence based working to take a firm hold'. p62.

An incremental programme has commenced since the arrival of Commissioner Hogan-Howe and strongly supported by the Deputy Mayor Greenhalgh. While it remains to be seen how far it develops, personally I conclude that it offers the best hope for this generation. Real reform will require more than dedicated insiders it will need outside in support that only an individual with a mandate from the electorate can bring.

The issue of focus also concerns the treatment of 'evidence'. This is critical, because as in medicine, it affects the confidence that the practitioner can have that the police 'treatment' to places, victims or offenders will work.

The difficulty is that there just over 100 randomised control trials—the gold standard—of what works where the influence of known and unknown variables can be confidently accounted for.

That leaves huge areas of everyday practice where the weight of evidence is not strong, but facts, audits and before/after studies exist, which are at least suggestive. And Stanko and Dawson's view is clear, (the)

> argument we propose, and the one we have done so throughout the chapter, is to move us away from the craving of achieving only 'gold standard' evidence—which of course can play a important role, but cannot routinely answer and arm officers within their daily work.

Many would agree that we have to use the 'best evidence' available. This does not devalue the gold standard, which they sensibly suggest should be applied on a risk-based approach, to issues of mental health, police restraint and vulnerable victims. It is salutary to reflect that police officers currently do not have validated tools, with a good standard of evidence to assess risks in relation to missing persons, domestic abuse or child abuse. The evidence we have is much stronger for places than people. We expect much from police officers; we should give them the knowledge tools to do the job.

So there is great work to do, and Stanko and Dawson offer us a real insight from a relatively privileged position of the challenge to reform policing in this era. Even a cursory glance at this monograph will make it clear to you dear reader that reform through an evidence-based approach is definitely not for the faint hearted.

But for those of you with the spirit to match the task, there is, thanks to this monograph, some evidence to help you navigate the barriers whether you are an individual officer, member of staff and visiting or embedded academic. I completely agree with their sage advice that EBP won't get traction from the periphery, although it will be occasionally rewarding. But, imagine if armed with this, you could be part of an organisation-wide plan, what you might achieve in protecting the public?

Sir Denis O'Connor

Executive Summary

There is a growing conversation between a number of players in the profession of policing. Those of us working in this profession for a number of decades sometimes grow weary of such talk about a new way of doing things. But these days we believe that there is a genuine change afoot, which also brings optimism. The discussion comes with the arrival of greater democratic transparency. There is an expectation that those with authority act with fairness and respect in the line of duty. There is also an expectation that a profession acts in alignment with best practice and best outcomes. And there are mechanisms to bring transgressions and failures of professionalism to the scrutiny of the public. All of these changes need better science and information to transform the business of policing.

This book takes the reader through a journey the authors have taken while working within and alongside one of the largest police services in the world. That journey is one which worked to embed an organisational approach to evidence-based practice across a variety of operational realms. These include place-based problem solving, working with vulnerable victims (in particular domestic violence, rape and mental health), cultural understanding for changing the ethos within operational units (high security, armed officers, neighbourhood officers), offender management, performance and intelligence analysis and the evaluation of many initiatives within policing and partnership working.

To change practice and behavior we must understand it. After over a decade working inside a police service, we offer this journey as a guide to helping you participate in a professional reformation. We describe the ways in which people act and behave within policing—from the perspective of insiders not outsiders—so that we help you learn to jump these obstacles, to bear the pressure to buck a risk-adverse and -resistant culture and to take individual responsibility to help steer a better course for better policing.

The journey starts from an appreciation of evidence in the business of policing. We acknowledge the tensions of welcoming science into a tradition of craft-based thinking. Yet we know that there will be a harder road to follow without recognising the usefulness of the logic of science, which in turn assists policing with the logic of problem-solving. To become a preventative agent, you will be expected to dig down and understand local problems (even if they are based in global illegal business). You—the thinking professional—will be harnessing the knowledge and expertise of those around you. And for us, the next and hardest part of the journey is to become committed to sustainable implementation of the learning from evidence-based policing work.

This book asks the reader to think about the relationship between evidence-based best practices, individual innovation and police improvement. There is still lots of skepticism about embracing 'evidence' generated from non-uniformed sources, because this implies a risk of getting it wrong or even trusting a source of knowledge that does not arise from the grounded experience of policing itself. Policing as a traditional craft prides itself on its knowledge, and its standards of practice often flow from its craft. Yet few of these standards of practice have been tested or are based on scientific study. That is not to say that what police currently do is wrong, but it is important now that we can test craft wisdom to do so.

This book offers insight into a decade of 'being' evidence based within one of the largest police services in the world—the London Metropolitan Police (the Met). Stanko joined the Met in 2003, and Dawson joined as her number two in 2008. Building a team of social science researchers, we influenced the way the police service created its performance information, and evaluated policy initiatives, operational decisions and activities and cultural change in its transition to neighbourhood policing. Not everything we did was successful in sparking immediate change. As we will demonstrate throughout, sometimes it takes a long time to bring about change and implement a different way of doing things. While police may excel in reacting to immediate need, as a profession, they are very slow to be systematic in a way which enables best practice to be a cornerstone, grounding and shaping decision-making.

The book is divided into three sections. The first section is devoted to getting you, the reader, to locate where you, your colleagues and your organisation are on a continuum of evidence-based craftwork. We emphasise the need for appreciation of the use of systematic studies of police interventions as the first hurdle in the adoption of better practice. The second section is a plea for an appreciation of the importance of implementation in the use of evidence and in its systematic application. Far too often we have wrestled with our uniformed colleagues who continuously wanted to stretch theory and practice and its use to situations where the integrity of the principles of what the evidence suggested was compromised. We strongly advocate feedback loops so that police officers learn from their own places for practice. Crime analysts and researchers have a critical role to play here. We need more information about how policing tactics or practice 'works' and works best 'here'. And we need to be able to make that judgment using the information that is routinely generated from police work.

The third section demonstrates how eclectic EBP research can be, and how it can influence even the way we test out the effectiveness of routine policing decisions. Drawing on studies of public confidence, place-based crime prevention pilots and 'nudge' studies of offenders' repeat offending, this section advocates that policing and police officers must make the space to work differently. This must involve some reengineering of the day to day, but as it harnesses the day-to-day information policing already produces, we believe strongly that it is possible to do. We know that finding the time to read, study, test ideas and discuss new ones in a fast-paced, reactive profession takes commitment as a police professional—whether you are an operational police officer or a civilian analyst/policy advisor. We hope to inspire you because we know that it is possible to generate systematic evidence in the throes of operational demands. But we do not underestimate the obstacles of cultural change, scepticism and difficulties you may experience along the way. This book offers you time to reflect, and hopefully to learn from our endeavours in the past decade.

Acknowledgements

We have been fortunate to work with a great and committed staff over the past decade in the Metropolitan Police Service, London. In particular we would like to thank James Bennett, Andy Higgins, Colleen Reddin, Daniela Wunsch, Jenny Norman, Liam Fenn, Sophie Geoghegan, Michael Keenan, Lynne Grossmith, Ubaid Rehman, Dan Shalom, Emma Williams, Barry Charleton, Jayme Johnson and Ben Linton. Betsy would also like to thank Rachel Tuffin from the College of Policing, Katrin Hohl, Ben Bradford and Jon Jackson who contributed significantly to the development of the work on confidence in the MPS. Paul would also like to thank Sergeant Chris Cook from the Metropolitan Police Service for his support and enthusiasm in particular around nudge theory. And to all the colleagues we have discussed many of these ideas, many thanks.

Contents

About the Authors

Elizabeth A. Stanko is Head, Evidence and Insight, Mayor's Office for Policing And Crime in London. For over a decade, she worked inside Corporate Development, London Metropolitan Police Service, establishing a social research function alongside performance analysis. In her first life, she was a professor of criminology, teaching and researching at Clark University (USA), Brunel University, Cambridge University and Royal Holloway, University of London (where she is an Emeritus Professor of Criminology). She has published over 80 books and articles over her academic career. The most cited of these works is *Intimate Intrusions: Women's Experiences of Male Violence*, published in 1985, and reissued as an ebook by Routledge in 2013. She has been awarded a number of lifetime achievement awards from the American Society of Criminology, most notably the Vollmer Award (1996), recognising outstanding influence of her academic work on criminal justice practice. From 1997 to 2002 she was the Director of the ESRC Violence Research Programme. In 2002, she joined the Cabinet Office, in the Prime Minister's Office of Public Services Reform. In 2013 she was a member of the Adebowale Commission on Mental Health and Policing. She is a fellow of the Royal Society of the Arts, a visiting professor at University College London (from 2014) and a visiting scholar at the Institute of Criminology, University of Cambridge. She was awarded an OBE for her services to policing in the 2014 Queen's Birthday Honours.

Paul Dawson is the Research Manager in Evidence and Insight, Mayor's Office for Policing And Crime in London. He is a Chartered Psychologist and Associate Fellow of the British Psychological Society. He previously worked for 4 years within the National Health Service followed by 5 years in the Home Office prior to joining the Metropolitan Police Service in 2008. He holds a Ph.D. in Psychology from the University of Birmingham investigating the empirical contribution of offender weapon-use within the analysis of serious sexual offending.

Introduction: Starting the Conversatio

This monograph starts from the perspective that may be different than many books and articles about evidence-based policing. Evidence-based policing is defined as 'using research and scientific processes to inform police decisions' (Lum et al. 2012). Lum and her colleagues (2012) have led a conversation about the disconnect between what is known from research what 'works better' when applied to policing, and the lamentable state of its limited use in the situations where police make decisions and plan action to tackle crime, to protect victims and to prevent offending. She and her colleagues are not alone to feel impatient about the slow uptake of systematic studies improving routine policing practices. Nearly every treatise these days discussing evidence-based practices in policing and the wider criminal justice system reminds the reader that we are at the beginning of this journey. Sitting aside this is a healthy amount of academic discourse on the challenges of working alongside policing culture from a scientific backdrop—illustrating issues such as police machismo, lack of receptivity and uncertainty as to the quality of evidence necessary to base operational decisions (Laycock 2012; Reiner 1992; Cope 2004; Chan 1997). Indeed, one aspect that shines through here is the lack of an agreed consensus in how to embed evidence-based policing, something in itself that could be hampering uptake. There is no consistent voice for police practitioners to fall back upon to help them be evidence based and act as evidence based professionals. The purpose of this book is to help fill this gap and to share our varied experiences on the use of evidence-based research inside a police service today.

We bring a decade of experience from working in a large metropolitan service to establish some basic foundations and conversations which appreciate university-based knowledge about policing and crime. We recognise that policing by uniformed police officers is a traditional, vocational and craft based job. Craft is critical to on the spot action. Police officers are in many respects walking arbiters of legal and other disputes for the public. Policing's history as a career and vocation is

E.A. Stanko, P. Dawson, *Police Use of Research Evidence*,
SpringerBriefs in Criminology, DOI 10.1007/978-3-319-20648-6_1

urated by its military and quasi-militaristic origins in the enforcement of state power and the resolution of disputes on behalf of the state. As a profession, its career structure has been traditionally open to those who largely grew up through its own ranks, its ethos and principles rising from an internal yet powerful relationship to controlling order on behalf of the state. As a consequence, the history of policing is also a history of managing access to criminal law and of resolving disputes often on behalf of those in political power. As the internal disputes in democratic countries rely less on lethal force, there are still many legacies for the roots of policing in an historical context of unequal power (in particular, in the UK reflect its origins in colonialism) and the influence of capital and its government, wielding power on behalf of the powerful and managing dissent, often of those less advantaged. This brief reminder of the historical origins of policing are important because they very much linger in today's understanding of the nature of policing. A culture of 'do what I say' and 'command and control' is not always compatible with a 'thinking' front-line led style of working. The welcome of new information challenging the 'way things are done around here', especially if non-uniformed personnel generated this information, requires a change in police culture. This is slowly arising in a number of places, but does not constitute a ground swell of change.

While policing culture has been explored by many academics, the study of police culture by scholars sought to explain and to connect the internal world of police to their external governing of the masses and consequently its link to the rule of law (Reiner 1992; Holdaway 2009; Loftus 2009). These explorations have attempted to give meaning to the work of policing through an examination of 'who' the police are and how they work/bond/play. Our approach is to take police culture seriously as a force to be reconciled with in not only mapping research evidence onto everyday practice, but in trying to alter the way the front line works given the evidence findings. In this monograph, we wish to find ways to open dialogue about this very strong (and stubborn) way of traditional working that is still largely closed to outsiders—even well-meaning researchers while at the same time talking about new ways of gathering and using evidence within policing. We agree with Lum and her colleagues that translation of knowledge generated within, about and for policing is necessary for its usefulness on the job. In an age of democratic transparency, we believe that this knowledge is critical. Policing is now having to explain its democratic 'offer' and its outcomes to a popular audience that increasingly demands fairness in the way police make its judgments. We wish to engage here with those who are attempting to find a way of working in a different—some term it more professional—way. If police can explain to the public that they indeed use a systematic way of approaching a problem (they think and act as professionals to get better results!), then this transparent logic that can be explained to the public at large is part of their discussion with democratic legitimacy. But this discussion mostly happens on the individual day to day level in the job. So we also wish to engage with those readers (YOU!) who may face scepticism in the job as to the usefulness of evidence-based approaches in the way you work. Especially if that sceptic is your boss.

Inroads to overcome such skepticism and generate evidence-based policing on the surface appear to be moving in a positive direction—indeed, there is no shortage of high profile advocates striving to promote a scientific approach and many others racing to find and to test tactics of managing persistent policing problems. While on the surface this would appear to be a planted and fertile ground—upon closer reflection the picture is far more complicated. The contradiction we highlight at the heart of this seemingly positive contemporary discussion is that evidence-based policing is not a new concept (Weiss and Bucuvalas 1980; Sherman 1998). Yet, it is only relatively recently that evidence based policing has built up this head of steam—but it is clearly not yet part of the 'craft' or 'toolbox' of everyday policing. Seeking to understand this gap and the receptivity of evidence into the policing profession is one of the more important questions we address here (see Lum et al. 2012).

This book attempts to move the reader beyond such traditional scholarly discussions around evidence based policing. It grounds the success of any discussions in the day-to-day reality of working within the police service itself. Rather than retread such old ground, the aim here is to share some of the unique successes, challenges and tensions we have encountered while working on the inside as police-based researchers. In our case—working as researchers *within* the London Metropolitan Police Service—*within* policing culture—*within* the very organisation that so many external academics and journalists have written about from the outside, has taught us more about 'what works' in receptivity than any article we have read so far.

Policing is undergoing a transition from its vocational working tradition as you, the reader, contemplate this text. And if you are a police practitioner, you are still likely to be dashing from pillar to post, supervising still chaotic ways of working that are not entirely compatible with armchair academics or even your senior colleagues who are frustrated with the inability of policing to get its act together to adopt a more measured, systematic way of working. The introduction of a science informed way of working is, we clearly acknowledge after a decade working inside a police service, in tension with its former (and still very strong) internal working cultures. Internal politics, short term appointments, performance cultures and the pressures to succeed, hierarchically based resistance to supervision and top-down challenges run continuous interference and undermine traction. This means that not only do you need to think about how you work differently; you need to influence the way in which others work too. Leadership is not merely demonstrated by adopting an expectation that those you supervise will use evidence based knowledge. You must also intervene in traditional supervision and risk adverse methods of decision-making that operate on the ground to steer the day job of doing policing and thinking about policing to anticipate and solve long-term issues. At the same time you need to find a way of harnessing new and emerging knowledge. Not an easy task.

Our perspective also takes seriously the view that the professional culture of policing largely protects and shields the uniformed officer from outside scrutiny. Getting into the inside workings of the uniforms, we suggest, is where you need to be in order to change practice. In so many respects policing is an 'inside' shop—few who do not wear the uniform understand the tensions between craft, reputation, pride and competence. Transparency is beginning to transform this, not least because the public sees some of the obstacles that police themselves have seen for many years. This should be one of the strong motivations to be more evidence based. We also acknowledge that policing skills are wide and varied. But we believe that there is a core of best information to build on to inform different policing problems (often solved by forming a special squad or unit) based in different countries. How crime is prevented, offenders are caught, victims are repeatedly victimised and so forth can be systematically studied. We need to use this work as the corner stones of change. We believe that there is a place to start using more scientific information that already exists, and this will aid better safety, public order, criminal justice outcomes and better service and protection to victims. The argument for evidence based policing suggests that improvement will be accelerated and people better served if police decision-making follows, is informed by, and is curious about what best practice and best outcomes look like. But this only will work if those applying best evidence also have an idea on how to influence others to work in a similar vein and know how to be flexible with best information to the circumstances faced at the time.

We absolutely believe a corporate or *whole-force* approach to embedding evidence based policing into *business as normal* and empowering uniformed and police staff is the right approach in bringing about such change. We do not feel that independent university courses working alone with relatively small numbers of motivated officers nor individual academic/police officer research will have the necessary impact unless they are linked to, driven or pulled together by a strategic narrative for change. As a result 'best practice' does not embed an evidence-based way of working within an organisation still uncomfortable to change. That is why we bring the lessons of organisational change to you here. In this way, we believe if change is to occur, it has to be compatible with the direction of travel for the center core of the organisation (yes leadership is important) and be underpinned by strategic need (yes, strategic thinking too is important). It won't gain traction from the periphery. Not from individual officers. Not from external universities. This support is critical but not transformational. This difference is key and underpins the approach we have taken for the past decade. Our end state is a presumption that we start first with understanding the problem, examining knowledge and systematic evidence, which then leads to a systematic and documented approach to solutions. And then we study the solutions (as robustly as feasibly possible) so that we can continuously improve. We believe that the full impact and requirements of such an approach is not fully understood, with the exception of a small number of pathfinders. We recommend you take a look at the New Zealand prevention first strategy as it sets out a corporate strategy in the journey for policing to become more preventative.

http://www.police.govt.nz/sites/default/files/publications/prevention-first-strategy-2011-2015.pdf

We also suggest that policing as a craft is under-theorised by scholars as a 'professional working culture' and as a consequence, and we will attempt to address this under-theorisation in this monograph as well. This is critical, we will further argue, because successful implementation of new ideas and of using evidence-based findings confront '*traditional*' approaches to the *'way we do things around here'*. Simply, we argue that training police officers to understand research or find the space to read about new research findings will be more easily accomplished in an organisation that has embraced innovation in technology, outside and open collaboration with partners and provides opportunities to consider strategic change through its leadership discourse that is open about the pressures of 'performance' and politics.

So let's change the conversation and see if we can work better together to accelerate the use of evidence-based thinking and research generation inside policing.

Foundations for Receptivity: Thinking About the Where and the How of Police Work

As someone with a desire to influence police practice, this section articulates some of the tensions you will be managing in applying the best academic and professional knowledge on the job. As we will demonstrate, conducting robust research is only the beginning of the story when thinking about changing practice within the police. Yet it is the beginning, and if we fail to fertilise the receptive ground we may find that we don't succeed with embedding change. We start with a number of principles that we feel practitioners and researchers must recognise in order to move forward together.

To change practice and behavior we must understand it. After over a decade working inside a police service, we offer this journey as a guide to helping you participate in a professional reformation. We describe the ways in which people act and behave within policing—from the perspective of insiders not outsiders—so that we help you learn to jump these obstacles, to bear the pressure from a risk-adverse work environment and to steer a better course for better policing.

Step One: Appreciation of Evidence in the Business of Policing

The growing discussion and popularity of the term evidence-based policing presumes there is a ground swell for its use across the policing world. But this is a new arena for many, and like many new other developments, it will take time for the transformation of the use of science evidence to filter into everyday policing. So for you—the interested reader—there is the opportunity to situate yourself, and your colleagues around you in this development.

This section of the monograph sets out a practical way of understanding where you and the police profession you are working with/within finds itself along a continuum of evidence-based/craft-based decision-making. It may provide some useful ways to argue for evidence based approaches to be adopted, so these principles are part of the wider narrative to support its use. Our springboard to discuss many such issues throughout this monograph arises from a similar survey to the one conducted by Lum et al (2012) to explore the perceptions of evidence based policing within senior staff many of whom had already been exposed to scientific thinking through their enhanced training as leaders in the London Metropolitan Police Service. This survey was conducted at the start of our own internal evidence-based policing programme initiated in 2012 at the behest of the Commissioner, drawing on many of the original questions Lum et al. (2012) used as our baseline. See Text Box 1 for an overview of the result.

Text Box 1. Case Study: A Survey of Senior Police Staff
We surveyed the top 250 officers (e.g., above Superintendent rank). The rationale was that these are the most influential staff and if change is to begin—it should start here. While the response rate was somewhat disappointing, (31 %, $n=78$), it is comparable to other online surveys. Indeed, the MPS's own internal staff survey has historically had a comparable response rate. Some may argue this demonstrates a negative attitude towards surveys;

E.A. Stanko, P. Dawson, *Police Use of Research Evidence*,
SpringerBriefs in Criminology, DOI 10.1007/978-3-319-20648-6_2

however, in such a large organisation staff may have reached survey fatigue, and others may note little changes following any survey. Two main themes emerged from the survey.

A fertile ground for evidence-based policing?

Around three quarters of respondents had heard of evidence-based policing as a concept. Respondents described that they saw the benefits of evidence-based policing as resulting in more effective working (96 %) and the ability to influence partners (63 %). This latter point is a positive—especially within the wider strategic context and the developing relationship between the MPS and its oversight body, the London Mayor's Office for Policing And Crime (MOPAC). This could easily become one of the major selling points of using evidence within a police setting—influencing stakeholders.

But can we see evidence being used …?

A somewhat startling finding was that 18 % of respondents stated that they would *not stop* a tactic if a researcher told them research showed it to be ineffective. This would seem to suggest a lack of trust in research evidence as a basis for operational decision-making. The majority (61 %) of respondents felt that experience was more important than scientific knowledge, with lesser (36 %) stating they had equal merit, and only 4 % thought that scientific evidence was more important than experience.

We wanted to learn more about the type of evidence the senior staff use to make decisions and presented many different shades of evidence asking respondents to reflect upon the regularity which they use the different types. We group these into three tiers. Firstly, the evidence we see used most frequently—within this, *'professional experience'*, with 95 % saying they used this on a *daily basis* to inform their decisions, *'the views of local staff'* (daily: 41 %); *'newspapers'* (daily: 24 %) and *'financial information'* (daily: 21 %). We suggest this indicates a focus on both personal experience and a reactive mindset influenced by opinion. The second most frequent tier used to inform decision making were some of the more robust shades of evidence. These were more likely to be used weekly or monthly. Here we see *'internal research products'* (weekly/monthly: 64 %); *'local analyst problem profiles'* (weekly/monthly: 71 %) and *'public or service user opinion gleaned from social surveys'* (weekly/monthly: 64 %). The final tier appears to be outside the daily workspace—but within UK local knowledge bases such as 'the MOPAC website', 'POLKA' (Police OnLine Knowledge Area, www.college.police.uk/What-we-do/Research/polka), 'academic journals', 'policing magazines', 'the Home Office website' and the 'Ministry of Justice website'—we see very, very limited usage. To illustrate, half of all respondents reported to have *never used* POLKA, 71 % never or rarely use Policing magazines and 65 % of respondents rarely or never use academic journals.

What the above case study demonstrates is that there are many different views about what ‘evidence’ is as well as what can be trusted and relied on for operational judgments. It is 2014 at the time of writing and there is momentum beginning to build within the Met, so we know that even during our tenure change is possible.

In a recent guidebook published by the US COPS programme, Taylor, Boba and Egge (2013) provide an approach to harnessing crime analysis for more directed patrol work. This guidebook too may help, but we think you also need to practice your own logic to convince others to follow your direction. We next turn to discuss where you think you and your colleagues are in the use of research evidence-based findings in operational decisions.

Where Do You Find Yourself and Your Development/ Engagement with Operational Decisions?

Policing craft is key to knowing how to use and to adapt the use of best practice in very different contexts. The problem of accessing better knowledge for policing is evolving and maturing as you read this. You may be reading this book on your hand-held device or your iPad or holding an old-fashioned transformed tree. It makes a difference whether you have access to better technology. Although the technology will not help you think, there certainly will be some impact on the access to and dissemination of evidence-based practice, made possible by technology—twitter, Internet repositories of synopsis of research and evidence-based advice, or even the ability to call a friend who knows (just like on 'How to be a millionaire' but without the monetary gain!) to help ground your judgement. But this technology is merely a tool to enable you—and the public—to be more reflective about police practice and craft-based competence. Knowledge about what works can be gained in a number of mediums, using them is up to you. In the age of transparency, bad knowledge (and bad research!) seems to go viral too, as examples of poor decision making hit headlines much faster than good decision making. The public may believe they know something about the way police work from reading novels or watching television, but they don’t know what it is like to make on the spot decisions or how to calculate the most cost effective deployment for pubic order events or for solving and preventing crime.

Those who ponder the state of the art of evidence-based policing though do agree that there is much, much more to do to bring together science knowledge and police craft knowledge. There is clearly a wide range of appreciation of the intersection of academic and practitioner based insight in the police service today. Such appreciation, James Willis (2013) aptly argues, is obstructed by the misfit between evidence-based and craft-based competence. Willis offers a very useful typology of the relationship of science to craft. See Fig. 1.

Depending on where you—the reader—locate yourself in the representations above, there will inevitably be tensions to manage. These tensions can arise because

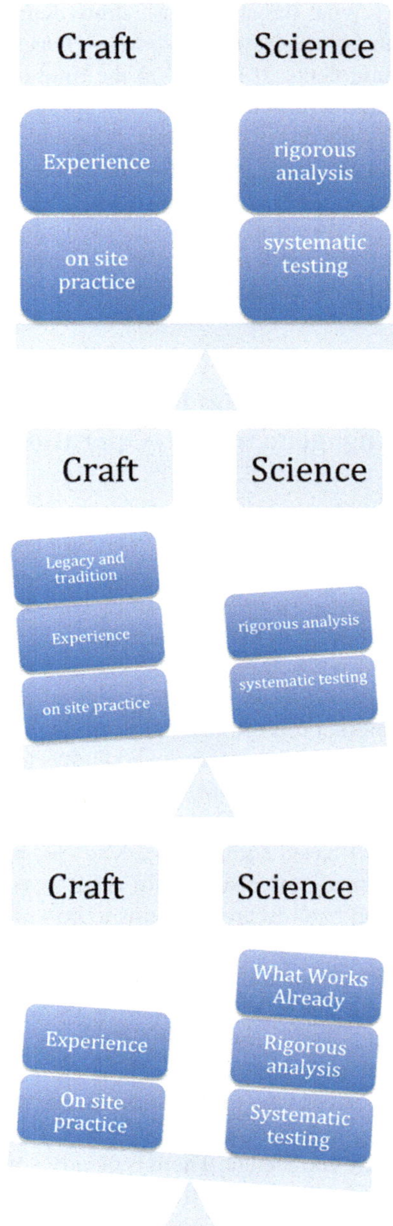

Fig. 1 The fit and misfit between craft and science

of the drag in progress caused by the way your police service is managed, the way it tasks operations, or the way it trains its staff. The lack of alignment of your thinking with the whole of the management of your police service, for example, is one. Any misalignment has consequences. So if you choose to work in an evidence based

Table 1 The potential strains between researchers, front-line and policy staff

Researcher views on policy/front-line staff	Policy views on research	Front-line staff views on research
Largely not interested in theory	Too academically orientated	Too distant/based within 'ivory towers'
Favour quick and dirty research over robustness	Too slow and not timely in producing results	What can it tell them about real policing?
Too concerned with spin or good news stories	Unaware of their pressures in producing results	Not speaking their language
Don't know how to use research	Too often doesn't give clear policy implications	Too often doesn't give clear practical implications

way, you may face skepticism from your colleagues 'in the police academy', your peers and/or your bosses when you try to argue for a different way of doing things, especially if you require newly inducted recruits to be familiar with the most up-to-date knowledge. Those you supervise may also be receiving contradictory advice, so your mentoring needs to support those inside who are trying to work differently. There is an implication that just having an evidence base tells us unequivocally something about how to apply it. Officers are wary of doing something differently, especially if there are disciplinary penalties for not operating according to standard operating procedure. We rarely hear how much effort it takes to move from a logical presentation of evidence to alter practice. As we highlighted earlier, there is no clear academic consensus or even much discussion about how to land evidence based practices into business as usual. We advise you to find out what your force is saying about the use of best practice, and try to influence the adoption of a better approach to align best practice with how your force is briefing or supporting your colleagues to do their job better.

Over the course of the monograph we seek to provide tips, insights and practical examples from our own experience that we hope will aid the reader to overcome many of these obstacles. Much of what we will be discussing will not involve standard operating procedures. But as the knowledge base extends, there will certainly have to take into account what the best academic evidence says. The use of academic evidence is already being introduced as the developments in the British College of Policing shows.[1]

There are many possible supporters to help rally the effort. Relevant here is the interlinked relationships between the 'researchers', 'front-line and 'policy' staff—with each holding different expectations towards research and often not aware of each others skills, needs or pressures. It is often no surprise that strained relationships occur in these settings (see Table 1, taken from Dawson and Williams 2009). It is through understanding such differences that we can seek to improve the relationships and ultimately the translation of research between these groups. These different perspectives are useful too. Research, when aligned to the policy and then

[1] http://www.app.college.police.uk/.

to practice, enables knowledge to be used and tested. But knowing where you are and where you want to go is part of the journey.

Example or thought exercise: How comfortable do you feel speaking to your colleagues (training, supervisory, specialist) about embedding a different way of doing things in the best academic research? Who are your allies, and can you start the dialogue within your department to change the way policing 'works' here? The best advice given to one of the authors (Stanko): work with those who 'get it' and build your base through this network—whether it be a virtual network or one that exists face to face with your colleagues. It helps starting with an appreciation of what you are trying to do, and how much commitment it takes to do so!

Step Two: Recognising the Usefulness of the Logic of Problem Solving

In many of our discussions with police officers from around the world, we acknowledge that policing as a public service is stuck in its fire brigade solutions to people's needs. Pressures and demands—coupled with decreasing public resources—are funnelled through an old style of working. Answering call after call for help, with a mix of experienced people responding to those calls, does not always add up to a formula for sharing best practice. Working to promote a collective understanding of why there needs to be a way of consolidating best practice for common problems enables a shared approach to the logic of problem solving.

Alongside the need for a 'whole policing approach', there are specialisms in policing and in policing knowledge—so many different silos have been created from knowledge empires that it is sometimes difficult to know what problem needs to be solved and what knowledge base to look to first. But before you express frustration about where to look, we would like to remind you that a major step forward is *to decide to use the logic of problem solving* to address the issues you see in your job (and help mentor those around you to promote appreciation of the usefulness of problem solving). This is not new advice, but it is advice that somehow has not yet been incorporated at the heart of police work. We realise that this has been part of the discussion about police improvement for decades, but it is not consistently embedded into business as usual.

Policing, we propose, as an occupation that has grown organically. Yet its knowledge base is largely experiential. It has been the subject for academic scrutiny and study, but much of the arising analysis of the profession tends to revolve around descriptions of what is termed 'police culture'. It is a profession that is largely reactive—to victims, events, chief officers and internal politics. Police forces shift and change depending on who the Chief Constable, Commissioner or Captain is (I've served under five Commissioners in my time in the police, and each of the Commissioners had very distinct styles, reflected in how open or closed the service was to public and political scrutiny). The profession is still largely suspicious of outsiders, mysterious and risk averse and with transparency the individual actions

E.A. Stanko, P. Dawson, *Police Use of Research Evidence*,
SpringerBriefs in Criminology, DOI 10.1007/978-3-319-20648-6_3

and organisational competence is being thrust into the public eye. If we aspire to be a professional like for example engineering,[1] one would need to harness knowledge of psychology, geography, physics, project management, supply chain business systems and other disciplines to build a bridge or design a new widget. So in terms of being evidence based about a problem, you need to know a lot about a range of topics to move a profession based on experience and personal style to one which has a knowledge base that can be consulted! Sometimes it helps being a specialist in an area yourself (for example I joined the service as an expert in working with victims of domestic violence). But it is impossible to be an expert across such a wide range of many different things, at least for most of us mortals. Policing needs a motley crew. So an appreciation of using problem solving to think in the round is the first step. Reaching out beyond your personal expertise also takes courage. There is still a fear of being blamed or disciplined if it all goes horribly wrong—and evidence doesn't guarantee success.

Police officers are often called on to solve many very different kinds of problems. It is because in their daily encounters with the public they are asked to 'do something' about a situation that seems beyond the ability of a citizen without police powers. The individual problem though is also part of a group of types of problems. Building on the logic of crime prevention is a way of thinking about 'success' or grasping an outcome-based approach: you are not only going to solve this problem but perhaps some other crime and disorder problems as well.

Problem-orientated policing has been around for over 20 years. There is a wealth of information available to support its use in a number of countries, to illustrate—the COPS site (see http://www.cops.usdoj.gov), the former Police Research Group based within the Home Office (See http://webarchive.nationalarchives.gov.uk/+/rds.homeoffice.gov.uk/rds/policerspubs1.html) or The Centre for Problem-Oriented Policing (see http://www.popcenter.org) all produce valuable guidance and tools for police problem solving. Scholars, the most noteworthy (and perhaps with the patience of a saint) is Herman Goldstein (1990), have worked to produce new knowledge to aid better thinking and results. Problem solving in policing, Taylor, Baba and Egge (2013) acknowledge, is still fraught with difficulty, despite the growing popularity in harnessing crime and other 'big' data to analyse crime problems. In a useful guide to assist police services to incorporate the use of crime analysis into their patrol functions, the authors agree with us that there are many obstacles faced in trying to produce useful and useable analytic products.

Problem solving is dynamic, and should be built into the DNA of policing. It underpins crime prevention and involves tactical menus that draw on the wider ingredients available within communities to sort out issues, which may be social, environmental or multi-agency in their solution. If you are a good problem solver, you need also to assure that those who work around you and who work in the same location reinforce the approach you have taken. That is, problem solving stretches beyond the confines of policing and into partnerships—as much of the literature in

[1] Stanko would like to thank Commissioner Sir Bernard Hogan Howe for this insight.

crime prevention attests. So you need to consider how to trust your own peers and/or staff as well as your multi-agency partners to understand the issues, and to ask uncomfortable questions if you are not convinced that your colleagues and/or your key stakeholders are taking a joined up problem solving approach. You also need to share your logic with your colleagues. More importantly, one of the ways of gaining insight about the problems your public are facing is to mine the kinds of problems that you are responding to on a daily basis in your local area. Know the business of local need. Once a kind of problem is identified, you can then see what kind of information exists in the evidence-based 'bank' that helps you address what you are managing.[2] For the record, we think the logic of problem solving is very much the logic of social science research and crime analysis.

During our decade within the Metropolitan Police Service, we devised a strategic approach to 'problem profiles' that drew on geography, sociology, victimology, offender-based analysis and performance data. For example, in setting a strategy for place-based policing, it is first important to know where the key places are for higher crime and disorder. Adopting a place-based strategy for preventing crime requires crime analysis products that identify spaces in the city where more crime/disorder is reported. The next challenge for individual officers is to select from a menu of tactics the right approach to tackle particular local problems. Consistent support for a wider level of activities including strategic partnership then addresses the drivers of a problem, and put in place levers for change. This enables the bigger picture of the problem of a crime type or a neighbourhood problem to be contextualised and key drivers to be identified so that middle managers and supervisors encourage the best local innovation to achieve the improvement. It is to this process we turn now.

Example or thought exercise: Can you identify a recurring problem that is happening in your local area? What are the identified issues? When, where and what is the problem? What data tells you this? What might be driving the problem? What are the enablers supporting better solutions? Who are your key stakeholders and partners? The next part helps you devise ways to demonstrating what your logic (or theory of change) is to work towards sustainable improvement.

---

[2] Readers are invited to consult the Global Policing Database (appearing on the London Mayor's Office for Policing and Crime from April 1, 2015 https://www.london.gov.uk/media/mayor-press-releases/2015/07/new-database-brings-together-65-years-of-policing-research-from).

Step Three: Digging Down and Understanding the Problem and Its Context

This part of the book advocates that you understand the 'theory of change' behind the use of tactics compatible with the problems you are facing. Even when we think we know the link between the policing tactics we choose and the problem solved this is often translated into 'improved performance'. Many of you will be working inside a police organisation or researching within one and have grown weary of performance regimes. For many reasons, the term 'performance' has become a dirty word in policing. There are many reasons why this may be so. There is great pressure on police managers to reduce crime (as measured by crime surveys and as measured by police's own recorded crime figures), but with little understanding that the drivers of crime have been robustly addressed to lead to sustainable improvement. Reducing crime in number may also reduce the crime problem. But this is not always the case. Understanding the problem, and focusing on the drivers of the problem, can help you not only conceptualise how to reduce this presenting problem but make observations about how other collateral problems might be addressed. Performance, achieving best policing results such as reducing crime, increasing victim satisfaction or making a city safer by reducing violent crime, can be driven through a focus on tackling the drivers of the problem. Performance discussions are in our experience too often a blunt instrument worrying about numbers, fed by a wary and cynical internal working culture working to get those numbers to go in the right direction. As we have observed, the very way policing is organised day to day—short-term goals, short-term assignments, siloed working—is not conducive to understanding the root causes of people's need for and use of the police, and such insight is critical for more defensible progress. To put it simply, insight is not (and should never be) limited to Chief Constable, Commissioner or Ministerial terms. Sustainable reduction is best and far more convincing to the public and any oversight board in a performance meeting. So while we advocate that you avail yourself of the best information available to manage a wide range of problems, what this book advocates is having a more viable and active process to make problem solving an integral part of your working life.

E.A. Stanko, P. Dawson, *Police Use of Research Evidence*,
SpringerBriefs in Criminology, DOI 10.1007/978-3-319-20648-6_4

Despite the very useful pool of resources available to policing, there has been very slow progress to using these systematically. But police cultures form a hard veneer of resistance to the embedding of a change of practice. Many scholars have observed internal police beliefs and practice that are not compatible with adopting advice that does not arise from individualised craft based learning. Reiner (2010:118) for instance says that police culture 'offers a patterned set of understandings that helps officers cope with the pressures and tensions confronting' them. Chan's study (1997:43) names the 'informal occupational norms and values' operating in a rigid hierarchical organisation. Bacon's recent essay (2014:116) summarises this influence as 'every occupational experience, every law, policy and training session, … is viewed through their [police officer's] cultural lens and woven into the social processes that reinvent and reproduce police culture'. Lum and her colleagues (2012) suggest establishing some 'institutional' levers to insert incentives for doing things differently. Problem solving using analysis and best practice rather than experientially based professional judgment challenges the flow of routine police work. You need to find space and solidarity with other folk to do this.

There is another factor we feel that mitigates against drawing on best research evidence on which to base problem solving considerations. In our experience, judgment of one's personal practice was often felt to be a criticism. Such criticism invokes a hyper-sensitivity—and the criticism of 'outsiders'—be they academics, politicians or stakeholder partners—sparking a defensiveness that deflects new learning. This is, we believe the sensitivity supported and produced by a closed, introspective organisation, one where there may be different 'cultures' but still closed to those outside the organisation. Such a defensive and rigid group culture may in part be a way of managing institutional/systemic anxiety—after all, change is threatening. Perhaps even more so if it comes from civilians or social scientists—many of which are young and have not endured the pressures of working inside. This internal sensitivity can create the deflection of changing practice. As others have observed, internal competitiveness drags progress. When someone is more concerned about retaining one's promotion prospects in the future, as well as being respected by one's peers, then risk taking is often limited. So you may find that you need to prepare one's peers as much as you can before drawing on knowledge 'outside' the profession, so ready your allies.

While the language of and pressure for 'performance' will inevitably lurk in the background, find a way to move beyond the confines of appropriate internal professional practice. For many officers this requires trust that the knowledge will be useful in the right context. Knowing who your allies are will help. Going further, building such relationships will be critical to encouraging the trust necessary for other colleagues to let go of some of the institutionalised defences and try something different. If you are in a leadership position, then we would go as far as saying that you have an obligation to improve the profession.

A seasoned police officer will already know some of the key tenets of what drives crime (for instance, particular places, repeat victims, persistent offenders, overlap between victims and offenders and so forth contribute to a steady flow of police business). And here is where your understanding of local problems and the context of problems will serve you well. The complexities of problems interface with many variations about victims (especially repeat victims), persistent offenders, problem places and routine and risky events. Evidence-based problem solving is not asking you to put aside this craft-acquired knowledge. It is asking to draw on additional knowledge—like the engineer draws from a wide range of knowledge to build a bridge—to devise and to use better tactics. Here is where science can help.

Knowing about crime performance (whether the problem is increasing, decreasing or staying the same) is not without benefits, for it sparks questions to about whether the problem itself changes. Rates of victimisation, reductions in the actual number of crimes or even an increase in a crime type does not tell you how the problem has changed. Use the everyday working environment as a 'teachable moment', where the logic of a police officer/police analyst comes together with that of a criminologist or social scientist to ask questions situating craft/professional logic while harnessing the approach of a researcher methodologist. We found this to be useful in working at the heart of one of the largest police services in the world for over a decade.

Example or thought exercise: Get hold of last week's (or last month's) performance report. See if this does more than report increases or decreases in crime. Can you find a way of improving the sharable knowledge of what is driving a persistent problem? And can you find a way of improving the product so that better, more insightful questions inform the tasking process? You are beginning to enter the world of the thinking professional!

Step Four: A Thinking Professional

To date, a few centers of excellence in universities have formed to coach policing into a new way of thinking and acting.[1] This is alongside a ground swell of innovation in social science which explores 'what works', under what conditions and why. Thinking like a professional means you think about what you want to change (in a presenting problem), why and what (or who) you can harness to assist.

You might wish to tap the wisdom from situational crime prevention, for instance, when a problem such as the theft of handbags and briefcases from bars and pubs appears on your watch. Or you may wish to test using nudge theory[2] to see if you can get the owners of the handbags and briefcases to take more responsibility for the care of their property. Each of these approaches has a 'theory of change' connected to it—this means that there is a hypothesis about the problem, learning to extract from other research about why the intervention might work, and a systematic approach to applying the learning and evaluating the outcome. This means not rushing to respond to a problem—but adapting a more considered (evidence based) approach.

Interventions can be aimed at a host of levels—each of which may have a positive (or not) shift in the problem. Of course, some interventions may cause harm and some may never even come to fruition (particularly the innovative ones)—that's why you need to have the best information to make this judgement. The often cited example of an intervention that does harm is 'scared straight'. This was an intervention used with young people to stop them being involved in crime in the 1970s. The so-called 'scared straight' theory of change proposed that bringing young people face-to-face in prison with offenders might frighten them from committing crime.

[1] In the UK, there is a growing base of like-minded policing folk to support the 'Society of Evidence Based Policing' or beginning to talk about the 'What works Centre for Crime Reduction' and what it offers.

[2] Nudge theory is a concept that brings together behavioural science, political theory and economics. See Thaler and Sunstein (2008) Nudge: improving decisions about health, wealth and happiness.

E.A. Stanko, P. Dawson, *Police Use of Research Evidence*,
SpringerBriefs in Criminology, DOI 10.1007/978-3-319-20648-6_5

The resulting follow-up showed that it did not prevent criminality, and actually resulted in higher rates of offending. Rather than prevent crime, the intervention exposed young people to offenders in such a way that made crime more attractive! Worryingly, scared straight in one guise or another still managed to exist in London in the year 2014.[3] So while there are good intentions (and you may feel that common sense was supported by 'fact'), this intervention should be avoided in your engagement with young people, particularly those on the cusp of offending. This does bring with it the sobering notion that 'good intentions' are not an adequate evidence base—something to bear in mind amongst the plethora of youth crime diversion schemes (e.g. boxing clubs, cricket clubs, music clubs) that the police and other partners appear to be regularly involved in.

So start thinking like a professional, using initially the 'holy trinity' of crime prevention: reduce the problems of re-victimization, problem places and persistent and problem offenders. Build these as strong pillars in the response to crime in your area (whether this be local, national or even global). And consider how to embed these using a clearer approach to understanding how those around you and those you supervise implement problem solving, the last and final principle of better evidence-based policing. Then draw on the evidence available on best tactics to hone in on improvement.

Example or thought exercise: Again, choose one of your (local) problems. What is the problem? Has anyone else had success solving out this problem? What kind of intervention are you considering and what's the theory of change for this intervention? Why should it work? What part of the problem does the intervention address? Does it tackle a key driver of the problem and can you measure the difference after the intervention takes place? Can you capture the outcome? Can you explain to others around you why this intervention made a difference? Now set up a simple performance product to document what you did! Now you can think about replicating your approach.

[3] http://www.standard.co.uk/news/education/schoolchildren-in-north-london-taught-lessons-on-life-behind-bars-9545131.html.

Step Five: Binding the Problem Solving—Implementation

Rigorous delivery and implementation of policing tactics are essential—and these issues do not always go hand in hand with policing culture. Packaging a collection of policing tactics into a strategic programme to design in more sustainable improvement takes the use of tactics up to an organisational strategic level. To put it simply, how a bundle of tactics is translated into a strategic programme and 'designed' and 'delivered' as business as usual dictates the type of results obtained. Initiatives without integrity do substantially worse than those with strong integrity (See Coulter 2010; Grove et al. 2012). This is a logical follow from the previous discussions around theories of change. However, throughout this monograph we refer to the concept of 'implementation' as a catch-all term for issues such as programme integrity, theories of change and designing and delivering programmes well. This is a whole systems approach to better policing. Such a term is used because our practical experience demonstrated to us critiquing police colleagues for lacking 'programme integrity' was not well received. Staff tended not to hear the former and focused upon the latter word and the lack of 'integrity' was sometimes seen as a personal affront!

Indeed, whilst much research and academic debate has gone into establishing and promoting 'what works', our reflection is that considerably less effort has been placed into ensuring that 'what works' is actually implemented as it should be. During our time within the MPS we have first-hand experience of this lack of recognition of integrity and implementation. Indeed, it has been something of an ever present shadow and going further, we argue that developing knowledge and/or training in programme integrity should be *as important* as building new research skills in the police. We believe this gap in ensuring integrity is one of the most pressing issues facing evidence-based policing and one that needs to be addressed as a priority if scientific thinking is to fully flower within the police service. Again, we seek to bring our insider perspective—beyond that of only emphasising the lack and need to incorporate integrity and implementation in the policing toolbox. Going further, implementation needs to be considered within the day-to-day activities of policing—something which is rarely as clean as a treatment or medical condition. In this way, we seek to convey a

E.A. Stanko, P. Dawson, *Police Use of Research Evidence*,
SpringerBriefs in Criminology, DOI 10.1007/978-3-319-20648-6_6

pragmatic approach to integrity, beyond that of 'cookie cutters' and seeking to understand the flex and bend underlying any programme and ultimately how much dilution to an evidence-based model is acceptable before it breaks.

While there are many guidebooks or texts around research design—many of impressive,[1] we feel that these are either too academically orientated or not attuned for internal Policing use. We have endeavored to make progress and develop practical instructions to enable practitioners to work through many of the issues we raise. This led us to develop our own research guide (see Supplementary Material) that takes a reader through the entire process with specific focus upon the design and implementation. Such practical guidance will be referred to over the course of the monograph as we discuss our efforts to promote systematic thinking to implementation. This new packaging of the *entire* research journey is important—to remind the reader, even well-known policing guidance to date (e.g. the SARA model: scanning, analysis, response, and assessment) we would argue does not reflect this whole process.

Example or Thought Exercise

After setting up a new policing approach to say problem places, how have you ensured that the menu of tactics were delivered exactly as how you wanted? Did you support staff with training about the approach? Did you provide staff tools and guides as to how to work? How can you ensure that staff collect the data you need to enable analysis? And can you document what difference the approach made to local people?

Now You Have Begun, in Summary …

We have emphasised some basic thinking around evidence based policing approaches. These include maintaining an appreciation of both the approach and the tensions within the police organisation in bringing these about. We know you will be facing some challenges in the way you wish to work differently. We feel that being thoughtful, organized and systematic will aid you in this journey. The next chapter argues why the craft of policing needs to be more consistent in its delivery. For many in the evidence game, this is often discussed as 'programme integrity'. Convincing professionals to trust the findings of research and to incorporate these into the way of doing business is a challenge even for medicine (cited as the leaders in the evidence-based world). Yet the resistance to the world of policing to consistency is as much about its legacies as a craft and as an internal culture as it is about best practice. It is in sharing these experiences that we hope you will understand why programme integrity is so important to improved policing.

[1] There are many other research guides and tools—see The Magenta Book (HM Treasury 2011) or the Maryland Scientific Method Scale (SMS) (Sherman et al. 1997) for a selection.

The Case for Programme Integrity in Police Craft: You Can't Do Science Without Being Systematic

Many voices aspire to promote evidence, research skills, and evaluation within the police, which have resulted in heated debates between academics in terms of methodological design and quality—with one of the main discussion points being the best type of research design (e.g. randomized controlled trials) sufficient to base judgements upon (Hollin 2008; Dawson and Williams 2009; Laycock 2012; Lum et al. 2012; Neyroud 2011; Laycock 2012). Essentially, we advocate searching for a balance between academic rigour and what is *good enough* for good policing.

A curious omission in most of these debates is the concept of programme integrity. We refer here to the use of a single tactic (for instance, sending letters to recently released offenders offering help to stop reoffending) or to a menu of tactics to achieve an objective (for instance, a suite of approaches to reduce reoffending). A programme with integrity ensures that an intervention is designed well and implemented exactly as intended. The more tactics involved the more complex the problem of aligning the way things need to be done. There should be a clear theoretical model, activities, aims, and be delivered in a specific manner to appropriate cases, likely supported by clear training, guidance documents and monitoring instruments. To put it simply, how a programme is 'designed' and 'delivered' dictates the type of results obtained—initiatives without integrity do substantially worse than those with strong integrity (Coulter 2010; Grove et al. 2012).

Indeed, as we outlined earlier, throughout our experience within the police we learned to modify our language and used the broad concept of 'implementation' as a catch-all term around programme integrity and delivery given negative reactions we encountered from officers when discussing a lack of 'programme integrity' (they sometimes focussed upon the lack of 'integrity' as a personal affront).

As such, academic discussions focusing upon gold standard methodologies or enhancing research skills of police are of value, but somewhat *incomplete* without first ensuring programme integrity. Here we argue that strong methodological

---

This section of the monograph draws from Dawson and Stanko 2013 "Implementation, Implementation, Implementation."

design or successful analysis in themselves are *not enough* to enhance the evidence base in the field of policing and far more needs to be done to ensure that the focus of any new research is based upon initiatives that have been designed and delivered in the right way. Without programme integrity, the risk would be that new well-meaning police research would be conducted on poor and ineffective programmes—damaging both the results and the motivation of police officers in their routine responsibilities to conduct research. *To put it simply, we do not want good research on bad schemes.*

We wish to share our experience of attempting to negotiate programme integrity and implementation through two case studies. These are examples where we have been asked to evaluate an initiative as objective insiders. We suggest that this approach is a different process than external academics or companies invited from the outside to assess success. We are in a privileged position of seeing all stages of development and are able to influence a systematic approach to programme integrity throughout the process. However, as we will show this is an ongoing challenge that raises core questions as to the culture of policing and role of researchers in achieving programme integrity. It also leads to those on the outside questioning the objectivity of the research, because it comes from within, a charge we do not accept. We feel strongly that it is possible to conduct high-quality objective research inside a police organisation. Indeed, this is the very offer of police-based internal research. The tricky part, however, about doing research or a programme evaluation from within is being willing to challenge the way the implementation is managed—and the inevitable tension that this brings to good working relationships.

Example 1: An Evaluation of a Reducing Gang Violence Project—The 'Pathways Initiative'

The London Pathways Initiative was a 2-year community-based, multi-agency pilot which aimed to reduce gang-related violence on three London boroughs. It was grounded in the well-evidenced Boston Ceasefire approach (Braga and Weisburd 2012). The approach (and theory of change) includes three interlocked elements: firm law enforcement, expressed community disapproval of gang-related violence (termed 'voice') and offering help to those involved in gang related activity a way out (an exit). The approach of Pathways was agreed in late 2007, followed by an overextended period of planning and consultation (see Fig. 1). There was instability in the participation of the local areas. During the project, one of the original three boroughs[1] pulled out to be replaced by another. The initiative requires explicit messages to gang related individuals to be delivered in particular ways. This means that the consequences of committing violence are stated explicitly by a number of criminal justice personnel and members of the community.[2] The first 'call-ins' were held in June 2009 and the final 'call-ins' in April 2010. We were asked to evaluate the initiative—and encountered many difficulties.

While a 'ceasefire' approach was broadly adopted, *changes were made to the core rationale* (e.g. no mandated large-scale call-ins, rather individual ones were used which undermined the 'theory of change' in the original design), and call-ins were implemented differently across boroughs. Practitioners were unclear which clients to work with and debated about the relative value in targeting low- or high-level individuals at risk of committing violence and spoke to us of the advantages of working with both. Indeed, the participant data we collected told us that there was a different way of selecting participants for the call-ins in each of the three locations. Out of the 161 participants, approximately one-third had no previous criminal convictions, although a sizable minority had relatively extensive criminal careers

[1] London has 32 local political jurisdictions called boroughs.

[2] See the work of David Kennedy (2011). Don't shoot: one man, a street fellowship, and the end of violence in inner-city America. Bloomsbury Publishing.

E.A. Stanko, P. Dawson, *Police Use of Research Evidence*,
SpringerBriefs in Criminology, DOI 10.1007/978-3-319-20648-6_7

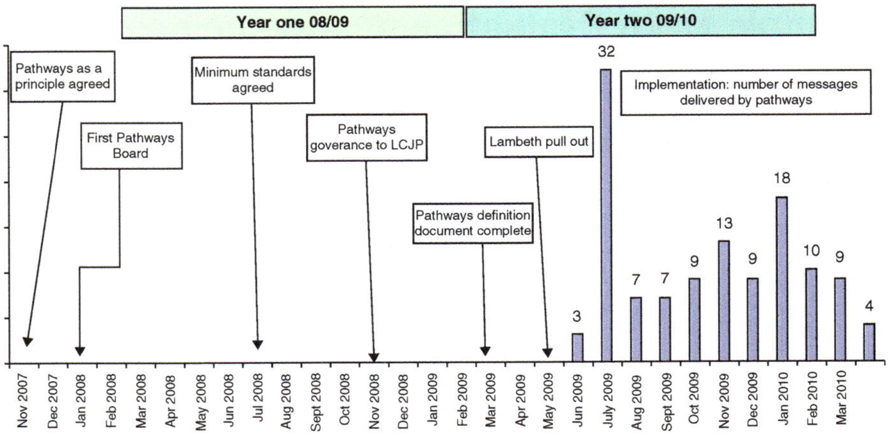

Fig. 1 Time line of the Pathways Initiative

(e.g. one in five had convictions for possession of a knife). Importantly, such issues undermined the replication of the Boston Ceasefire model and critically damaged programme integrity. There was no 'replicable' Pathways approach per se, something that effectively ended any hope of a robust outcome assessment. We were continuously asked whether Pathways 'worked'.

A variety of conversations we had with the project team warned them that the scientific approach was undermined, and especially when our final research report was delivered, these robust discussions continued. There was no way we could comment on whether what happened had 'worked' (in the interest of rolling out best practice) because there was no common best practice adopted. There was no robust clarity on what was being tested and how this aligned to best practice. The messages we were delivering around the outcome of programme were understandably unwelcome. The issue here is that designers did not fully embrace programme integrity and instead had a greater focus on capturing local need and adapting the original evidence-based model (e.g. the Ceasefire approach) to their particular setting. This balance is very important. Of course, there is a need to capture local variation, but we wonder how much actual value such changes to the core model made, set against the damage to integrity? This balance becomes even more pertinent given the current 'localism' agenda of the UK coalition government, where there is a commitment to 'what works' without a clear steer on what programme integrity might really mean in terms of replicating 'best' outcome at a local level.

We are not advocating a 'cookie cutter' approach—that is far too simplistic. Police officers not only need to know which tactic works best, but they also need to know how to supervise and monitor the delivery of success that is compatible with the theory of change. Yet, there needs to be an awareness as to the *limits or flex* to an evidence-based model, and how much dilution to a model is acceptable before it breaks. This lesson is not just one arguing against local adaptation. It is one that requires the local adaptation to articulate what the theory of change is behind the adaptation. This is a fundamental change to the craft of policing because it requires systematically laying out the approach in advance and an even more nuanced and pragmatic approach to working with programme integrity. As we discuss throughout this chapter, practically, we argue that this requires additional emphasis on programme management and integrity so as to establish a policing culture that is more conducive to routinely achieving desirable outcomes. This is an add-on to discovering and using the best tactics that 'work'. It requires additional skill around implementation. As can be illustrated by the timeline, there was little time to evaluate the initiative, and there was no documentation as to the rationale why some locations choose some pathways over others. In the end, our evaluation was not an evaluation of the 'Boston Ceasefire Model', because there was no test of the model.

Example 2: Evaluating a 'Diamond' Approach to Integrated Offender Management

In 2008/2009 there was a compelling case for developing a 'Justice Reinvestment' model of offender management within London. That is, shifting resources from universal financial budgets to needy geographic areas. Drawing on the 'Million Dollar Blocks' concept developed in the USA and Integrated Offender Management (IOM) principles, London launched the Diamond Initiative, which set out to manage non-statutory short-sentence prison release offenders in some of London's most challenging areas. This was designed and launched deliberately as a landmark scheme and was supported by approximately 11 million pounds for its 2-year duration. It was conceptualised as London's first IOM scheme and was the subject of high political and ministerial interest. We were asked to undertake an evaluation of the programme. Reflecting this importance the authors were determined to design an evaluation that would stand up to the firmest of academic and political critiques. The Initiative was explored through a variety of 'theories of change': (1) Staff matter for success; (2) offenders want to change and will accept offers of help; (3) offending declines if (1) and (2) work well and (4) the outcome costs the taxpayers less. These were tested through an evaluation that considered both the implementation and impact (on staff awareness, offending and economic cost benefit) of the Diamond Initiative using a variety of methodologies. These were the following:

- Four waves of online staff surveys designed to capture the changing views of practitioners over the entire lifespan of the scheme.
- Two waves of qualitative staff interviews (72 interviews in total) to dig deeper into implementation issues and capture key learning from a representative sample of multi-agency staff.
- Two phases of qualitative offender interviews (58 interviews in total) to reflect the experiences of those participating in the scheme.
- A quasi-experimental study of reoffending, a level four on the Maryland Scientific Method Scale, using data from the Police National Computer to compare the proven offending behaviour of Diamond referrals to 'a statistically well-matched control group', over a 1-year period.

E.A. Stanko, P. Dawson, *Police Use of Research Evidence*,
SpringerBriefs in Criminology, DOI 10.1007/978-3-319-20648-6_8

- A cost–benefit analysis of Diamond, comparing the economic benefits generated by the scheme, in terms of the cost of crimes averted, against the set-up and running costs of programme.

In an interesting add-on, overseeing the evaluation and acting as a 'external' critical friend was a specially selected group including some of the most well-respected names in UK academia, e.g. Prof. Mike Hough, Prof. Brian Francis and chaired impressively throughout by Sir Anthony Bottoms of the University of Cambridge. On a purely methodological note, we greatly benefited from the board's quality assessment and advice on the research, particularly on our statistical approach to generating the control group. Given the calibre of the attendees such feedback was priceless. But, it is perhaps the wider role of the board that was of more value upon reflection, acting as a buffer to many of the political and process demands and providing the evaluation on site verification and peer review. This was a high-profile initiative being tested for governmental policy. This raises the wider problem of how pressures impact 'any' innovation and how these pressures are managed. At one point we had major doubts and called for and were granted a wholesale verification of the case management system due to our concerns about the robustness of the data. Without this our final evaluation would have been in doubt.

After 2 years of rigorous analysis, the headline finding was there was no evidence of reduced reoffending—the political measure of success for the programme. Comparing the Diamond cohort to a statistically matched control of 'similar people, released from prison at a similar time, within similar areas', revealed no differences in offending behaviour (e.g. proven reoffending, survival, amount or seriousness of offending) in the 12 months subsequent to prison release. Both groups offending levels were exactly as we would have predicted using the Probation Service's Offender Group Reconviction Scale (OGRS[1]) classification.

Our methodology allowed a tracking of staff and offender views over the course of the initiative, and it is through these we can generate insights into the reasons Diamond may not have achieved better results in the short term. Getting inside the 'black box' so to speak—key in assisting decision making and understanding results. These can be summed up as:

- The time it takes to implement a new initiative (e.g. the set-up had to overcome a number of obstacles such as information technology, accommodation, training and staffing).
- The support offered to meet offender need at a local level (the research highlighted gaps in partnership working in addressing the needs of offenders), which meant that offenders may have wanted to change but had little access to help that addressed their specific needs.
- The cultural tensions in staff from different agencies working together (ongoing working tensions between police and probation staff were evident and could

[1] The Offender Group Reconviction Scale (OGRS) is a regression-based model for predicting likelihood of resanction based on static factors such as age, gender and criminal history. It has been used by probation and prisons in the UK since the late 1990s.

have been avoided by more staff training on roles). However we found that views of staff began to converge as time went on.

- And critically, the time frame for the success of the initiative and an outcome evaluation just 1 year following set-up. Two years for a new project is rather short in our view. The short term given to follow up for evaluation was a requirement of the national politics. Professionally, we should have had started the evaluation clock ticking later, at least 6 months into the programme, when some of the early start-up teething problems would have been overcome. We could not therefore measure impact or cost benefit in this way because there was not enough time to enable us to realise the full outcome of the programme.

So, in essence—we were robustly evaluating an expensive initiative, hampered in the early stages by implementation issues, which matured in terms of multi-agency delivery but never fully reconciled 'working tensions' between the police and other partners. The point here is that each of these issues could have been anticipated in the design at the beginning, with a sound respect for why programme integrity is critical to success. These findings establish many of the key challenges that need to be recognised and have to be taken very seriously in order to deliver any effective offender management initiative (and we suggest other initiatives that require new ways of working). The main results of the evaluation are documented in our final report (Dawson et al. 2011). Here we share the lessons of programme integrity and what we have learned from our experience of doing evaluation from the inside of a police service.

Evaluation in the Eye of the Storm: Reflections on the Diamond Evaluation

It is difficult for readers to fully comprehend the internal and external stakes that were on the table with this evaluation, for the practitioners, the politicians, the programme and the researchers. Practitioners and politicians courted media coverage, and after our first-year report many expected to read about a successful solution to a worrying problem of high reconviction rates for a significant group of offenders. But the government changed (yes, politics does matter). Following this change of government, Diamond took on the additional political weight of proving IOM as a concept and that of the 'rehabilitation revolution'. There was an additional national IOM (excluding London) external academic evaluation at the time but was only able to explore 'process' and not 'impact' (Senior et al. 2011). Because we had skillfully negotiated access to data from the inside (and knew the ins and outs, pitfalls and frustrations of managing such data sets), we had information about reconviction of the very sample population that was in the political debate about offending.[1]

Our scientific findings, ratified and scrutinised by our external academic advisory group were disappointing about reducing reoffending. No one, least of all ministers and senior police officers, wanted to hear about our 'no impact' results and our calls to embrace the learning from within the research. No one wanted to hear about how—over time—staff learn to work better together. But the promised results were in the public domain and thus became front-page headlines. This is in stark contrast to Weatheritt's (1986) 'doomed to succeed' comments, whereby in-house police evaluations are placed under pressure to report favourably. There were a variety of negative press reactions to the scheme, ranging from 'The Sun' (… '*an 11 million pound scheme to get jobs to go straight has no impact*') to the local evening London newspaper, the Evening Standard. Our evaluation was delivering unwanted and potentially embarrassing news (there was no quick win against reoffending) and

[1] Indeed, our Diamond evaluation is still regarded by many as the best IOM research to date and we continue to be invited to speak at the UK and international conferences to share our learning and methodology.

E.A. Stanko, P. Dawson, *Police Use of Research Evidence*,
SpringerBriefs in Criminology, DOI 10.1007/978-3-319-20648-6_9

many police (and other staff) felt it reflected badly on the job they did. A thick skin became a prerequisite when delivering such results. Many commentators highlight how the police perceive conducting research as 'risky' to their careers (Lum 2014). Our work on Diamond can be seen as a prime example of this, albeit with the risk played out in the national media. Yet, our evaluation was one of the strongest of its scientific type and given the methodology the results could not be questioned. Quite a predicament—we delivered a methodologically innovative piece of research and challenged our own organisation's ideas.

The Diamond Initiative had more integrity than the Pathways Initiative, but if anything, we experienced a different implementation problem. The start-up of Diamond was '*too quick*' and there were many teething problems that had to be overcome post its very public launch (e.g. IT, appropriate staffing, resources and supervision). This speed could be feasibly linked to the political pressures Diamond was under to succeed. We also suggest that there is a lot to be learned from this about what we call the 'point-zero' of an initiative; by this we mean that the point at which an initiative is fully operational. The question for any evaluation is at what point to mark the 'beginning' of an initiative for purposes of analysis so to avoid teething problems so only the effect (and not the start-up) of the programme is under study. From a practical perspective this raises the interesting question as to when clients should be 'taken on' to such an initiative: if this is done too early within implementation there is the danger that clients will not receive a service as it was designed through its 'theory of change'. This also raises the acknowledgement of the pressure of 'political' policy research and the need to receive quick-time results 'within' either the career of sponsors (e.g. political appointments, Senior Police sponsors) or the current Ministry of Justice 'Payment by Results' framework[2].

Our evaluation did not as far as we know cause any additional harm. But it did result in police officers being wary to trust a methodologically sound evaluation that gave them bad news. What happens if the police officer made an operational decision that caused harm or went wrong? Why is such news felt to be a failure if the tactic is shown not to work? We have learned that such negative results are treated as bad for people's careers, and not as occasions for learning. Negative research results, such as that from the Diamond Initiative, can be just as useful as positive ones—if there is a strong learning culture in the policing organisation. We would argue that such a learning culture does not currently exist or is very immature. This we further suggest explains the continued perceived 'risk' of academic research and the reception the results from the Diamond initiative received from both media and many internal police officers and staff. We had to remind people continuously that robust findings are learning opportunities! One must have a steely exterior to withstand the pressure to promote only good news. Some may shy away when there is no guarantee that evidence-based research is really risk free, especially if you are going to end up being castigated in the national media.

[2]Payment by Results was introduced by the UK Government and broadly refers to providers of offender management receiving payment upon meeting demonstratable results based upon proven reoffending.

In the case of the Diamond Initiative, the move from such disappointment to learning has been very slow (some police still refuse to cite the work because of the perceived failure of the programme). However, this Diamond evaluation placed London far out ahead of the UK regarding offender management primarily because it was the only IOM scheme to receive a robust process and impact evaluation. Lessons learned were clear around the importance of staff understanding of the 'theory of change', programme integrity and implementation. The challenge for the MPS was how to embed the learning in the next stages of their work on reducing reoffending. The challenge for ourselves subsequently was how to spread the word around 'programme integrity' within an organisation that was still reeling from the results.

Influencing Programme Integrity from the Inside … and Widening the Conversation Outside

As described, the experience of evaluating Diamond was a rich and eventful one. Our roles as researchers working on the inside changed and broadened out as a result. To illustrate, within IOM we participate in various IOM board meetings (both inside the MPS and across London and national government) and seek to influence the development of policy and practice in offender management—far beyond what a traditional researcher or external academic contractor would. London's IOM, in particular, is only now, many years on from the final Diamond evaluation attempting to take on board our results in terms of design, basing an approach in the use of evidence. However, much of this can be attributed to our personal influence and way of working. While a positive, this does demonstrate the requirement of internal champions (and personalities) with the courage and craft to insist upon the use of scientific evidence driving change from the inside. Working on the inside brings with it contact to the wider struggles of internal (police, local and national) politics, the ever-changing landscape of personnel and personality of those who occupy key roles in the advancement of knowledge, and the very real pressures of limited time in an atmosphere where crime performance dominates the culture.

Upon completion of the Diamond evaluation we were regarded as the MPS's Centre of excellence regarding evaluation. Ironically, many doors opened largely due to that work, and as a result we now hold a wide portfolio of evaluation design and work[1]. We have now moved our entire unit to the Mayor's Office for Policing And Crime, but that has accelerated the appetite for evidence-based policy with measurable outcomes. Unfortunately, the shadow of wrestling with integrity has been a far too routine within all the evaluations of initiatives we have conducted and likely of those we will conduct in the future. Each of these examples could be written up in a same manner to Pathways or Diamond. Our challenges have ranged from

[1] Dawson and Stanko have since moved to the Mayor's Office for Policing And Crime, and continue the work of evaluation from this new work site—giving us access to wider partnership conversations as peers.

E.A. Stanko, P. Dawson, *Police Use of Research Evidence*,
SpringerBriefs in Criminology, DOI 10.1007/978-3-319-20648-6_10

communicating the over-focus on the statistical strength of comparable statistical tools as opposed to ensuring compliance of a Predictive Hotspotting trial, to the frequent issue in defining clear outcomes and the ever present partnership tensions and difficulties in finding common data for evaluating complex multi-agency innovation. There are too many examples that could be described here that illustrate the problems in establishing robust "what works" internal studies. These are far too frequent to be labelled as chance. This is an area that requires serious attention and discussion among those working in the arena of evidence-based policing. We wonder how many broader policing or policing/university research studies capture the whole journey, as opposed to focusing upon evaluation design or statistical analysis.

Our broadened role brings with it risks in terms of how we challenge given our greater involvement during these formative stages of new initiatives. It takes courage to say that something 'doesn't work' especially when you are employed within the very organisation promoting the approach. We return to our comment earlier about requiring 'thick skin'. Police officers are not typically trained project managers and present a 'can do' attitude, as opposed to the more considered/systematic approach required to ensure integrity of a programme in order to deliver a robust outcome evaluation. This observation provides key insights into perhaps why integrity has not been fully appreciated within evidence based policing. As a working unit inside, we consciously decided to not take on evaluation requests unless a tactic or initiative can demonstrate explicit consideration of integrity (we have standards!). To do so would simply not be effective use of the resource devoted to insight that leads to financial and operational decisions. This has not always made us popular, but we regularly highlight to all that listen the need to ensure integrity and effective implementation is not just a matter of evidence-based policing. It is a comment on whether we feel we can make a contribution to the wider policing knowledge.

One of our attempts to counter this was to develop a mini-research guide available to police officers that covered the value of 'gold standard' methodologies, but only once programme integrity and implementation plans had been established (see Supplementary Material). Our role as insiders has been to attempt to empower staff to create an active feedback loop and place the tools within the toolbox so to speak. Our guide consisted of many steps in which we attempted to set out the basics in a simple manner: defining the problem, scanning and learning from the current evidence base, designing the initiative, planning the implementation, planning the research and then 'doing' the tactic or the programme as effectively as possible and as intended—all prior to the research analysis. Checklists asking key questions at each stage supported this. Such a tool requires not only motivated officers whom are willing to spend the time to work in a new way, but also that are in a workspace that allows them to forward plan and (ideally) design initiatives in the right way, as opposed to being rushed to produce results or parachuted in to ongoing initiatives that have not been set up well. The guide can be used in such cases—the questions stand—but best value would be gained using the guide starting from step one. The tool also has benefits for policy or other advisors in commissioning, understanding or critiquing research they are presented or overseeing.

Final Thoughts on Programme Integrity

Rigorous design and implementation of police tactics are essential—and this does not always go hand in hand within a policing culture that prefers only good news. We cannot emphasise more strongly that there should be as much effort into assuring best implementation as possible, so that when people select 'what works', they understand 'how it works' and 'how to implement' it so that it might work again (of course with attention paid to context). Evidence-based policing should not be limited to 'only' identifying and then deploying proven tactics to a particular problem. This is too simplistic—we do not believe in 'magic bullets' or 'cookie cutters' to solve and to reduce crime. Policing research will likely never be as clean as a 'treatment' in a medical context, given the wide range of social and economic issues involved. Policing initiatives are often administered in 'dirty' environments and this needs to be acknowledged in the design and implementation—but not to the point where the core of either the theory of change or the integrity of delivery is undermined. In this way we seek to convey a pragmatic approach to integrity, seeking to understand the flex and bend within any programme. Critical next steps should focus on training and embedding this learning within policing, as this is the route that will ultimately deliver better outcomes through improved integrity. The next part offers the way you can promote and influence the way your police service works.

Embracing the Challenges in Professionalising the Police Profession: Learning to Work with Evidence Differently

In this last part we wish to discuss how you influence the take-up of your promotion of evidence-based thinking and strive towards overcoming some of the more prominent challenges you may encounter. We bring our insider knowledge again to the fore and reflect on those challenges we feel need greater airtime if evidence-based policing is to genuinely take hold. These challenges are broadly outlined as follows:

- The challenge in making effective research influence policing
  One of the most successful evidence-based bodies of work we conducted to influence the Metropolitan Police is that focusing on confidence in policing. This body of work is nearly a decade in the making, and has set out a corporate approach to improving the Metropolitan Police's relationship to the people of London. Although there is empirical evidence about 'what works' to drive public confidence, this work is more of a road map for building confidence (that is, understanding the theory of change) than a collection of 'what works' tactics. We will take you through the journey. The first step was to produce the robust research and link it strategically to the overall success of the legitimacy of policing in London. The second step is a hard lesson: effective use of research from our experience takes a long time to embed. Robust evidence-based findings don't quickly find their way into business as usual. Here we will talk about a place-based crime prevention trial Stanko conducted 8 years ago. We are just now getting back to these lessons with an eye to embedding place-based principles for crime prevention in London as routine practice! A critical boost to this embedding is that the research has been at the heart of the police service's key targets for improvement. But despite a central stage in the Metropolitan Police's performance regime, there was little understanding about why confidence or place-based crime prevention was so important to the delivery of good policing.
- Nudging the police: rank and parochial stubbornness
  Conducting research on the inside of the police service brings with it contact with a variety of internal politics and winning 'hearts and minds' requires more

than recruiting senior police to support a research-evidenced direction. Working with peers and those you supervise also need to be transformed. There are many practical nuances involved when conducting research inside the police, and you need 'surround sound' support. Here we offer an illustrative case study of encountering such internal issues and attempting to 'get the basics' right in terms of producing best/better evidence.

- Devoting time to persuasion: communication and challenging business as usual

  We firmly believe a corporate approach to embedding evidence-based policing into business as normal is the right one and the one we have taken for nearly a decade. This raises many issues, both at a corporate and individual level, and we are unclear as to whether the full impact and requirements of such an approach are clearly understood in terms of how much time and effort this really takes. In this section we highlight the need for persuasion, and that time for this needs to be woven into the transforming of policing craft.

  A warning: this part of the journey may take much longer than you think. We share these experiences not to exhaust you, but in the hope that our experience will not be repeated by others! We want the progress of change to speed up. So, we will go through these challenges we faced in turn, flavouring each with case studies and practical attempts/tools that we have developed in our attempts to overcome these.

The Challenge in Making Effective Research Influence Policing

The research into public confidence in policing was driven by the fact that we were keen to move beyond crude 'tick-box' notions of citizen satisfaction, which offer ways of thinking about the direct contact between citizens, policing and their police. The work on confidence asks 'why' police are important in democratic relationship between citizen and state. For many police officers, trying to enhance the legitimacy of their organisation can often seem an abstract or over-complicated endeavour, especially if they believe their core concern should be around improving tactics to fight crime. Of course, these are not mutually exclusive aims. The research on public confidence is trying to influence the way police interact with citizens. There is considerable evidence that trust in the police is important for the rule of law in itself. Trust in policing is linked to concrete citizen behaviours—cooperation with officers, compliance with the law and engagement in informal social control—that would help police to achieve their crime fighting goals and benefit officers by helping them doing their own jobs better (Tyler 1990; 2007; 2011; Tyler and Fagan 2008; Tyler and Huo 2002; Sunshine and Tyler 2003). Tyler's procedural justice model (Tyler 1990) is now being discussed in a number of countries for its link to improved policing. He firmly links the fairness with which police officers exercise their authority to public trust, police legitimacy, and the types of behaviour listed above. Interpreted in its broadest (and perhaps most optimistic) light, procedural justice theory holds out the promise of a criminal justice system predicated on a more cooperative and less coercive relationship between police and public than it often seems to be the case (Hough et al. 2010). And it does so by placing the relationship between police and public centre stage. Perhaps we in Western democracies have underestimated the damage distrust does to public cooperation with public institutions. But following the disorders in London in 2011 and in Ferguson, Missouri, in 2014 we are less dismissive of its critical requirement.

This section of the monograph draws on Stanko et al. 2012 A golden thread.

E.A. Stanko, P. Dawson, *Police Use of Research Evidence*,
SpringerBriefs in Criminology, DOI 10.1007/978-3-319-20648-6_11

The theory of change at the heart of this work is Tyler's procedural justice approach. By using procedural justice as a lens through which to view police-public interactions we can begin to find meaningful ways of providing answers to questions from police managers about what they should 'do' about public confidence, answers that paint a much clearer picture of the dynamic relationship between the police and those they serve (see Stanko et al. 2012; Jackson et al. 2013). But rather than a discrete list of tactics, some are beginning to approach the need for enhancing police understanding of procedural justice to improve how police 'are'.

Arriving at a theoretically and empirically robust definition of public confidence was inevitably only half the story, but it is a strong position from which to start. The opportunity to apply these concepts empirically emerged through a series of London-based studies using the rich data sources accumulating in the MPS (Bradford and Jackson 2010; Bradford et al. 2009; Jackson et al. 2009; Jackson and Bradford 2010; Hohl et al. 2010). A collaboration developed with academics and the work emerged in various public fora. Bradford and Jackson (2010) offered an approach to trust and confidence which included three different components (a) judgments of police effectiveness and the ability to do "the job" of dealing with crime and catching criminals, (b) judgments of police fairness when dealing with people, and (c) judgments of police responsiveness to the wants and needs of the community. Their research has found that believing (or trusting) the police to be effective is less important in predicting overall public confidence than more socio-relational aspects of shared values and the fairness of interpersonal treatment. Jackson and Bradford (2010) propose that above all, *overall confidence* is based on trust that is rooted in a particular social alignment between the police and the community. What appears to be most important to people is the idea that the police understand, share and act upon people's concerns, and that police officers have the right motives when acting (whether this be on their behalf or in ways that may curtail or even remove their freedom). This social alignment seems to be founded upon public assessments of the ability of the police to be a 'civic guardian' that secures public respect and embodies community values (Loader and Mulcahy 2003). By demonstrating its trustworthiness to the public, it follows; the police can strengthen its social connection with citizens and thus encourage more active civic engagement in domains of security and policing.

As the theoretical insight began to mature, we were left to find practical ways to introduce ways that senior officers could both persuade and hold officers to account for their influence on public confidence. All of the theoretical and conceptual refinement had to be translated into a performance regime that would spark activities that would encourage the police to do something different in order to gain more public confidence. As a first step, the MPS set about adopting an approach to public confidence that was continuously monitored by its own contracted out public opinion survey, with measures for overall confidence and the above outlined three constituent drivers, public engagement, fair treatment, and police effectiveness in dealing with crime. A fourth driver—dealing with antisocial behaviour—was also included in the performance data the Met received on a quarterly basis.

The most pressing question for police themselves to address was perhaps this: are there tactics police can use to foster confidence by the public? The most obvious route to improvement is via the police's direct dealings with individuals. That interactions between officers and members of the public are key moments when public confidence is 'tested' against police actions seems a reasonable suggestion. But to link personal contact with attempts to enhance public confidence implies the belief that officers *can* enhance trust through the way they deal with those they encounter. That is, we must think that police can behave in such a way during encounters that individuals leave those encounters with a more favourable opinion than that held before they met. Unfortunately, the empirical evidence for such a claim is mixed. While virtually all studies find that negative or unsatisfactory contact with police can have a strong negative effect on trust, positive effects from satisfactory contact prove to be much harder to identify. Skogan (2006) has characterised this as the asymmetrical effect of contact—negative effects overwhelm positive ones. Others, by contrast, insist that contact experiences can have uplifting effects on trust (Tyler and Fagan 2008). But for the police themselves, such academic 'facts' are discouraging, particularly within a performance regime that expects improvement.

Bradford et al. (2009) examined this issue using the MPS's Public Attitude Survey. While the cross-sectional study meant that firm causal conclusions were not possible, enough hints were found that positive effects from contact were possible to suggest that, while asymmetry certainly exists (the negative impact of poor encounters is always likely to be greater than the positive impact of good encounters) the situation is not hopeless. Splitting confidence into three dimensions as outlined above, the academic work found that the statistical effect of contact on public confidence in police fairness was at least somewhat symmetrical. This enabled us to demonstrate that procedural justice-type effects might be found in the UK and that it was at least possible that police could improve public opinion for the better if they improve the way they interact with people.[1]

The message about the way officers and the public interact was becoming clearer. The way officers treat members of the public is a vital element in any attempt to improve trust and confidence, if only because such efforts would be seriously undermined if large numbers of people were coming away from encounters with police officers feeling alienated, upset, angry or disappointed. The salience of this issue is multiplied by research suggesting that vicarious experiences of police activity—what we hear from other people—can be as important in opinion formation as personal experiences (Miller et al. 2004; Rosenbaum et al. 2005). The effects of unsatisfactory contact with police may well ripple out beyond those immediately involved. These findings are embedded in the MPS internal briefings on confidence and a key part of the debates during routine 'performance' discussions at the highest level of the organisation. They are now routinely part of the conversation that the

[1] On a related note, when looking at the national picture in England and Wales, Bradford (2011) found that the (small) positive effect of contact on 'overall' confidence may have grown since the 1980s, which, among other things, could suggest that people are more 'open-minded' about police, and more ready to change their minds as a result of personal experiences (alternatively, it might suggest growing fragility in opinions, as once settled views of the police, positive or negative, become destabilized and more subject to change).

Mayor's Office for Policing And Crime—the Met's oversight body has when reviewing overall policing for London.

The most practical and currently most intensively used tactic to contact the wider public in London are letterbox leaflets. The MPS Neighbourhoods Teams used this information to think about how to disseminate (aspirationally) newsletters to all households on each of London's 108 areas (serving 624 wards in a city of 8.4 million people) on a regular basis.[2] What appears to be most important about any direct communication with the public is its contents and the message it sends. The police show through a local message that they know what the local issues are, understand them and report back to the community about the outcome of the actions they have undertaken to tackle these issues. By doing so, the police demonstrate to the public that they take the local concerns seriously, act on behalf and in the interest of the local community by addressing them, be transparent about their activities and show themselves accountable to the public in reporting back to them (Wünsch and Hohl 2009). In collaboration with academic colleagues, we tested this approach by conducting a quasi-randomised experiment in seven London wards. Overall, the newsletter had a small positive impact on confidence in the police (Hohl et al. 2010). But this does not mean that this information has led to the distribution of newsletters as business as usual.

At the same time, not all communication with the public is good communication. In an unpublished, internal MPS pan-London follow-up study, we found that newsletters can also backfire. If people feel the issues addressed in the newsletter do not reflect their concerns and make the local police appear oblivious to the 'real' problems in the local area, or seem incompetent in responding to them, then a newsletter can have a negative effect on trust in police engagement and overall confidence in the police. This is an important finding as it underlines the importance of the newsletter being creditable and part of a wider policing strategy aimed at building trust and confidence. Newsletters can be an effective multiplier and catalyst of police work on the ground. What they cannot be is a cheap substitute for engaging with the public, finding out about local concerns and responding to them.

These findings on police use of newsletters add support to the idea that while the key components of trust and confidence (effectiveness, fairness and shared values/interests/community engagement) are related, they are also empirically distinct and differ. Evidently a one-off newsletter was not enough to change people's beliefs about police fairness and procedural justice in direct encounters, especially when some people and some communities have a history of being treated unfairly. Yet, the experiment provides good evidence that leaflets, if done well, can be a creditable and effective way for the police to influence public confidence. The work fed directly into the MPS's strategy for public engagement and has become part of a continuous feedback loop in implementing approaches to improving public confidence. It has also been used in performance reviews with senior leadership teams in local areas. It is now taking center stage in the work of the Mayor's Office

[2] Initially newsletters were disseminated on a quarterly basis. However, this has waxed and waned over the past years with different financial resources and changes in leadership commitment.

for Policing And Crime in its engagement opportunities with local areas. All of this has taken years from the original bespoke research to influencing the conversation, so our advice is to be patient and impatient, changing the relationship of policing to the public takes a long time (this is an important lesson for those introducing democratic policing in areas of the world where conflict or inequality has been rife).

Turning to the application of the learning about the importance of place in crime prevention, one of the authors (Stanko) led an initiative where eight small town centres identified as high-crime areas were identified for bespoke problem-solving activity. This initiative drew on a number of principles from the situational crime prevention literature. First, that crime clusters; second, that a focus on the worst places led to limited displacement and can improve high-street areas; and third, that the police are but one of a number of partners in this crime prevention approach. However, what the initiative did require was a good problem profile on each of the areas, and a commitment to translate the problem into a multi agency solution. The initiative ran for a year. The performance data clearly demonstrated a clear improvement especially in the reduction of violence associated with the night-time economy, with no displacement effects. But the initiative was not translated into business as usual. Eight years later, Stanko is repeating the exercise, as the approach to crime prevention was not embedded in the Met, nor in performance discussions, and not in training. Even with evidence from our own force, incorporating best practice into operational policing decisions was not made routine and an expectation.

Nudging the Police: Rank and Parochial Stubbornness

Nudge theory (Thaler and Sunstein 2008) has been embraced by a range of UK and US politicians and a plethora of other public and private organisations, drawing inspiration form the world of psychology, behavioural science, political theory and behavioural economics and in a gross simplification—can be described as the study of decision making and how these can be improved. In respect to the UK, the 'Behavioural Insight Team', (BIT) (aka the Nudge Unit) was formed in July 2010, with a main drive to *test, learn and adapt*—and to transform how government thinks about public policy and enable citizens to make better choices for themselves.

There are numerous striking examples of the use of 'nudge' within public policy, everything from improving the accuracy of male urination (see Thaler and Sunstein 2008) to increasing organ donation (Cabinet Office 2013). As of early 2012 something peculiar was occurring—the term 'nudge' was being spoken of *within* the Metropolitan Police Service. There are many potential reasons for this, the main being the sheer level of interest that the BIT were generating at the time.[1] There were others reasons of course, and while at this time there had not been a crime reduction-specific test of nudge, there were transferable tests that inferred the value of nudge within a policing environment. To illustrate, there is a powerful nudge piece demonstrating that we can improve the payment of court fines when messages are personalised (Cabinet Office 2012). It could be argued this was the beginning of nudge moving towards the criminal justice system.

Whatever the reasons, it was clear that the practical application of such work within a wider offending framework seemed to have piqued the interest of senior leaders at the MPS, especially at a time when Police budget cuts were pressing and efficiencies were in demand. It also sat comfortably along the concept of Evidence Based Policing and police professionalism. To drive this forward the MPS organised a crime prevention seminar in May 2012, where senior staff from the BIT spoke, amongst other well-known and highly respected academics (e.g. Ken Pease, Sylvia Chenery).

[1] http://www.theguardian.com/commentisfree/2011/sep/19/government-nudge-unit-behavioural-insights-team.

E.A. Stanko, P. Dawson, *Police Use of Research Evidence*,
SpringerBriefs in Criminology, DOI 10.1007/978-3-319-20648-6_12

A range of senior MPS staff attended (e.g. an Assistant Commissioner and Chief Superintendent) clearly indicating that the MPS means business in the incorporation of scientific evidence into policing.

Soon after this event, we in the Evidence and Insight unit were tasked with facilitating a specific 'nudge' trial with offenders. This was an exciting opportunity; there had not been a specific crime reduction nudge trial before in UK policing. As if to illustrate the potency of such a project, the Behavioural Insight Team kindly offered their expertise in the design.

In summary, the aim of the trial was to test whether how we communicate with prolific offenders can have an impact upon their crime reduction and explore what might be the most impactive style of letter. The design was proposed to be a randomised control trial, with prolific offenders being randomly allocated to different types of letter at one consistent point in their career. Evidence and Insight designed the letters in collaboration with the BIT (who kindly provided critical advice and quality assurance). The design of the letters incorporated previous research as to how people read letters, attempted to make the letters as straightforward as possible and we even took guidance as to the best type of font to use, for a group that may present reading difficulties. The letter conditions were as follows (see Supplementary Material for the designed letters):

1. No letter (e.g., baseline).
2. *Standard text* regards the MPS/enforcement.
3. *Standard text* AND *personalised* (e.g. the individuals name).
4. *Standard text* AND *Personalised* AND *Support* (e.g. some support agencies and phone numbers to contact).

Initially, four boroughs were in scope to be included in the trial, although on communication with senior Police staff (the MPS lead for Integrated Offender Management) this was expanded to cover a total of 13 boroughs—a genuine boost that would enhance sample size. So, the signs were altogether positive: a timely and evidence-based concept, the support of high-ranking centrally based senior police staff and the support of the 'nudge' experts in the BIT. Building upon some of the learning from our previous experience in terms of promoting programme integrity (Dawson and Stanko 2013), we even designed an 'implementation guide' aimed at supporting police practitioners through the actual trial and logistics (e.g. the practicalities of using our randomiser, data capture sheets, research process charts and so on—see Supplementary Material). The stage was all set for an innovative crime reduction 'nudge' trial. Unfortunately, the trial as described progressed no further, and the reasons why, we would propose, are telling in understanding more around the uptake of evidence within the Metropolitan Police Service and reveal some of the lesser discussed practical challenges conducting research within the police.

The problem arose when we sought to communicate the trial to the Borough Commanders[2] and received what we can only call an 'unenthusiastic response' from

[2]Each Borough in London has a Borough Commander—also known as the rank of Chief Superintendent—is the head of Policing within the Borough.

many, mainly due to boroughs already having their own offender 'letters.' Interested in what type of letters were already being used we collected examples. We were surprised by the considerable variation between the letters across boroughs, no corporate oversight, no consistent branding, no standardisation and no evidence base behind the letter designs used. Neither did we find any evidence of results analysis being conducted to inform or assess the impact of the letters being used. To add further complexity, in our view some of the existing letters were potentially harmful almost taking a 'scared straight' approach—(i.e.) '*We want to ensure that your entire neighbourhood will now be working against you.*' Indeed, one letter we obtained that was sent to certain types of prolific, acquisitive and other offenders was merely a newspaper clipping on a A4 paper (e.g. no MPS branding) highlighting an article describing the MPS arresting and convicting an individual following the use of traceable liquids and a decoy car—with text underneath stating that as '*you have previous convictions… we thought this article … would be of interest to you.*' Needless to say, such designs are all absolutely counter to actual 'nudge' theory. In pursuing our nudge trial we were opening a proverbial 'can of worms.' Upon reflection, there are a number of key elements to this piece that ought to be expanded upon.

Firstly, this serves as a strong example regarding how communication flows through and down large organisations such as the MPS and where the blockers (and therefore potential facilitators may be). While senior staff were willing to promote and sponsor the trial, such willingness did not, as a result, routinely filter down the hierarchy. This raises a wider question around how typical instructions filter down within a police service as large as the MPS. Our experience in this example and in other research is that the 'middle management layer' (i.e. Inspector–Superintendent) can be the most difficult group to get on board and whose lack of participation can be keenly felt, partly as this level are able to act as a conduit to the 'rank and file' of police PCs. Indeed, even within our own corporate MPS staff satisfaction survey[3] only 21 % of respondents reported to have confidence in the leadership provided by senior leaders. This is not specific to our middle management group, but we would suggest does demonstrate a clear 'gap' between (centrally located) senior staff and others (borough and locally based).

Secondly, we would argue that this demonstrates an almost *parochial stubbornness* to not forgo their own borough letters (despite the lack of evidence in the design or analysis to indicate success) over the use of letters developed in collaboration with the BIT. What is interesting in this example is that many boroughs were already writing to offenders, we doubt these letters derived out of nudge theory, but nonetheless, the concept was already in practice. A clear willingness to innovate practice was evident. For us, this also raises the conscious awareness (or not) of scientific evidence that police staff have or need to have. In some cases police may explicitly use scientific evidence, but in others they may be only implicitly using it, that is using techniques that are based upon evidence but they may not know

[3] Evidence and Insight oversaw the internal Staff Survey of Police staff—distributed to all staff for completion.

(or need to know) of the scientific underpinnings. In either case, the contradiction we highlight was the decreased motivation to use specifically developed evidence-based letters over the ones currently being used and developed by local staff. This echoes previous commentaries in terms of police staff being somewhat unresponsive to evidence or taking a 'doing what you feel is best' or using professional judgment in making decisions.

Turning back to these two issues, much research has been written in terms of scepticism of research within policing culture (Lum et al. 2012) and we would not disagree with this for a moment. However, as we are attempting to illustrate, there are more subtleties that need to be factored into such discussions in order for genuine progress to be made. It is far too simple to scold policing culture as being unresponsive to research. Issues such as rank, localism and how the trust of local staff outweighs the trust of others, such as centrally based researchers or leaders, are all essential ingredients that need to be factored in when promoting an evidence-based approach within the police.

Returning to the nudge trial, subsequent to the initial hurdle, we argued that all such written communication to offenders should be standardised across the MPS, and that a small number of corporate templates could be designed—which themselves become a new 'nudge' trial within the MPS as to how we communicate to offenders. We remain optimistic that a nudge trial with offenders will soon take place and at the time of writing are advancing a design testing differing levels of personalisation (e.g. using photographs) within letters received by offenders.

Devoting Time to Persuasion: Communication and Challenging Business as Usual

It was made clear in England and Wales by the Neyroud review (2011) that a path was being set with the explicit aim of shaping a future 'professional' vision of policing. On behalf of the new incoming Police Commissioner, we created a visionary project that went far beyond our previous isolated attempts[1] to embed evidence in the MPS. Our programme had a number of broad strands (i.e. governance, locking together performance and research, training and organisational support), each focussing upon a separate issue with the totality of the programme being stronger than the sum of its parts.

We absolutely believe such a corporate approach to embedding EBP into *business as normal* and empowering police staff to create and to draw on best knowledge is the right approach. We believe that an internal transformation is critical. This should be supplemented with independent university engagement or bespoke university courses (typically) working with relatively small numbers of motivated officers or individual academic/police officer research. However, our experience is that the benefits of improving individual officer knowledge are very rarely driven or pulled together by any strategic organisational narrative. As a consequence, there is no corporate commitment to embed the systematic use of or encourage the generation of evidence within the police organisation. This difference is key and is core to how we work. We believe if the delivery of policing is to change, it *has* to come from the centre of the organisation and be supported by strategic vision—not an agitation from the periphery. Neither individual police officers, nor charismatic academics bring about the necessary foundations for evidence-based working to take a firm hold. And any commitment brings with it the need for more mature discussions around evidence-based policing. In this section we draw on the survey featured in the first part of this monograph and add some case studies where we have been successful in introducing the use of research-based evidence into the decision-making frame.

[1] Our previous attempts to embed evidence were not as comprehensive, e.g. such as attempting to develop research groups or evaluation training.

E.A. Stanko, P. Dawson, *Police Use of Research Evidence*,
SpringerBriefs in Criminology, DOI 10.1007/978-3-319-20648-6_13

The Need for Standards of Evidence Within Evidence-Based Policing

An early starting point in our survey design on receptivity of evidence-based policing was how we went about describing what evidence was and the different shades of evidence that we could present to staff. We took a broad approach in attempting to establish evidence as a type of information (Briner and Rousseau 2011) that people use to inform their decision-making. Our survey listed concepts from 'professional experience' to 'academic journals' to 'web-blogs[1]' to 'The Home Office Website'. All of these to a *degree* are evidence, but the quality varies and there lays the rub. As we saw, one of the most striking findings from the survey was the daily use of professional experience, and regular use of newspapers and public opinions to make decisions. More formal types of evidence (e.g.) bespoke problem profiles and in-house research were used, but less frequently. Academic journals, the UK's College of Policing's knowledge sharing portal POLKA,[2] Home Office and Ministry of Justice websites were very rarely used.

This is not purely a semantic discussion around the term 'evidence'. Especially within policing, formal evidence is often seen as fingerprints, DNA and the like. The danger that we highlight for evidence based policing is that the term 'evidence' in itself is far too broad brush and can refer to many types of evidence. There needs to be clear definitions and standards of evidence established and promoted to staff. Ultimately, this means that police staff will need to be able to critically assess different sources of information/evidence and make decisions accordingly—and be flexible when so called social science 'gold standard' evidence is not available. There are already models that seek to grade evidence that can act as a starting point to facilitate discussion within policing (e.g.) the excellent Scientific Methods Scale for evaluation design (Sherman et al. 1997). However, the

[1]We acknowledge that there are some excellent blogs out there for research and important issues 'see mental health cop'. http://mentalhealthcop.wordpress.com/.

[2]This is a knowledge-sharing site that is open only to police officers, police staff and those who work in Policing and Crime Commissioners' offices.

E.A. Stanko, P. Dawson, *Police Use of Research Evidence*,
SpringerBriefs in Criminology, DOI 10.1007/978-3-319-20648-6_14

authors have previously commented upon the need to compromise aspects of methodological design and not *only* limit oneself to gold standard designs (Dawson and Williams 2009).

This balance between quality and compromise is an important debate for police research. Gold Standard research can be time consuming, difficult to design, often requiring large samples (Gondolf 2001; Harper and Chitty 2005). Quasi-experimental, the next step down, can require a sophisticated statistical counterfactual. These methods pose questions and challenges for experienced academics and evaluators. In this way, it is not realistic to promote 'gold standards' as the *routine approach* for police learning. As researchers we encourage adopting the most robust feasible approach, tempered where necessary with caveats. After all, we are working with not against police or other customers and indicative research is an important tool in generating insights. It is unacceptable to not conduct research just because 'gold standards' cannot be met (Dawson and Williams 2009). Of course, this balance applies most when an impact assessment is actually what is required. It is equally not feasible (from a resource or financial position) to conduct high quality impact assessments on *every* initiative or tactic. Prioritisation is key. For those high-profile or innovative pieces, of course robust evaluation should be the norm. However, performance frameworks, better understanding of the problem, understanding how something has been delivered, public opinion capture, staff opinion capture and other insights may be more valuable (and actually be what is required).

We present one model from Evidence Based Medicine[3] known as the GRADE (Grading of Recommendations, Assessment, Development and Evaluation) model (Guyatt et al. 2008) to start more pragmatic conversations within policing (see Table 1). This model goes beyond methodological strength and draws upon other

Table 1 The GRADE model

Quality of evidence	Definition
High	Further research is very unlikely to change our confidence in the estimate of effect. • Several high-quality studies with consistent results • In special cases: one large, high-quality multi-centre trial
Moderate	Further research is likely to have an important impact on our confidence in the estimate of effect and may change the estimate. • One high-quality study • Several studies with some limitations
Low	Further research is very likely to have an important impact on our confidence in the estimate of effect and is likely to change the estimate. • One or more studies with severe limitations
Very low	Any estimate of effect is very uncertain. • Expert opinion • No direct research evidence • One or more studies with very severe limitations

[3] http://www.medicine.ox.ac.uk/bandolier/painres/download/whatis/ebm.pdf.

layers of evidence. There are four levels of evidence ranging from very low (expert opinion or no direct research evidence) to high (several high quality studies with consistent results). For any model of evidence to be effective within the police we suggest it needs to incorporate these lower shades of evidence that we see used (blogs, newspapers, expert opinion) and encourage the aspiration to use the higher level shades of evidence. Any such model would need to be supported by clear definitions, knowledge repositories and training to allow staff to quickly access and understand such evidence.

What Should Be the Balance Between 'Craft Experience' and 'Scientific Evidence'

One issue we encountered in the survey was the *balance* between craft/experience and scientific evidence. Our respondents clearly felt that accumulated policing experience should play a greater role in decision-making and was used daily to inform decisions. We consciously connect this to James Willis' discussion of the tensions between craft and evidence-based policing. Personal experience is of course essential, but in terms of decision-making can be impaired by the numerous types of cognitive bias (Stanovich and West 1998). In broad terms, cognitive biases are ways of thinking that can lead to inaccurate judgements, recalling past events incorrectly or illogical interpretation (e.g. searching for information that confirms one's preconception or assessing ambiguous information as positive to one's interests).

We also suggest that reflecting upon this balance is only half the story. Indeed, we wonder whether it is ever feasible for the police to routinely '*use*' scientific evidence throughout their entire decision making process. This raises the risk of testing ones own professional judgement. The authors argue that it is more valuable to explore '*where*' scientific evidence really *ought* to be used, especially in these relatively early stages of evidence-based policing. That is, we suggest an incremental approach to change, instead of speedy whole-scale change running the risk of implementation failure. If this is the case, the real question becomes which topics within policing *need* to use scientific evidence. The authors suggest that an effective starting point to such a discussion would be a risk-based approach. By this, we refer to areas whereby there exists clear risk if police actions fall below an expected standard. For example—issues around how best to understand the intersection of mental health and the police (e.g. restraint and/or police custody) or the investigation of crime involving vulnerable victims are both clear candidates where scientific evidence should be core to the craft.

E.A. Stanko, P. Dawson, *Police Use of Research Evidence*,
SpringerBriefs in Criminology, DOI 10.1007/978-3-319-20648-6_15

Training, Time and Technical Ability to Allow Breathing Space for Evidence-Based Policing

Throughout the chapter the concept of learning has been a common thread—as a sister piece to the survey documented earlier, we also sought to assess how much academic evidence the major MPS training providers[1] used in the design, set-up, running and generation of feedback of the training they provide. We would suggest that there is a huge gulf between what policing as a profession has come to understand 'training' is for the craft of policing and what academics expect in terms of learning 'what works' and how to document systematically the impact of a tactic or approach. Our work in the Met showed us that the traditional approach to 'training' left training to the realm of moulding craft experience. We explored this by working with the Met's training providers and each completed a self-assessment. The self-assessments showed three main challenges.

- *Limited awareness and use of scientific evidence*—training providers talked about being evidence based but this predominantly referred to professional craft experience, with scientific based evidence on 'what works' featuring infrequently. There was good practice in terms of the use of environmental scanning or subject matter experts in training design, but it was not clear to what extent this ensures the use of the most robust scientific evidence.
- *No systematic approach to embedding scientific evidence*—the process of reviewing and updating courses were often iterative with the responsibility falling on individuals to update their own courses sometimes in their spare time. Unless officers or staff are studying for higher degrees, they have limited access to the latest academic knowledge.
- *Practical barriers*—a range of challenges were outlined such as budget cuts, trainers delivering a range of courses, the high amount of administration and generally felt there was not enough time to search for or use evidence.

[1] Leadership & Learning, Crime Academy, Public Order and Firearms.

E.A. Stanko, P. Dawson, *Police Use of Research Evidence*,
SpringerBriefs in Criminology, DOI 10.1007/978-3-319-20648-6_16

In our opinion, training is severely limited because it presumes it is training a craft and not drawing on knowledge that also exists in journals, systematic reviews and other scientific learning on policing. We feel there is the need for new specialist topics which address the 'science' side of learning, such as programme integrity and/or even research methods. Perhaps more worryingly, we are not convinced that police training is currently fit for purpose in the new world, drawing on, and developing the best evidence. The wider questions facing policing—that of productivity, culture, professionalism and other key topics—are utterly dependent upon appropriate and effective training and learning.

Neyroud's (2011) review of police leadership and training calls for a transformation in the culture of learning in the police service, in such elements such as continual professional development. This could result in a revamped training and learning curriculum and even include public involvement in developing or delivering the training. Numerous organisations could play a role here. In the UK, the College of Policing, The 'What Works in Crime Prevention Centre', oversight bodies such as Her Majesty's Inspectorate of Constabulary (HMIC), universities and others could all contribute at present and in the future. Even more research—specifically addressing the outcomes of training—is required to bring policing training into the twenty-first century.

A Demanding Job: Why Don't We Have the Time to Read?

We would argue it is an uphill battle to embed scientific evidence within a police force for a variety of reasons that have already been documented. As if these were not enough, there are other far more simple challenges that can easily be overlooked—something as simple as the daily demands of a busy (and sometimes not so busy) policing shift. How prepared are officers to find and spend valuable available time to scan, read and think about research issues? It could be argued that the College of Policing's knowledge portal POLKA[1] was a step forward here as a repository and an attempt to being communities together, but as the results of our survey showed, few reported regular usage. While in the UK there is a growth of the Society of Evidence Based Policing attempting to skill-up police officers and generate research, the meetings draw relatively small numbers of motivated officers. To bring a cultural change new ingredients need to be introduced to the entire craft of policing, especially the profession's own training capacity. The simplest enabler is to encourage officers and staff to find time within their busy routine to read about the latest research and evaluation findings. This could also be assisted by training, peer support (pressure), management systems and investments, integrating research into the assessment and promotion process. There are even online search engines (e.g. Google Scholar) that can provide automatic research updates around key topics.

The reviewer of the first draft of this book felt that this next idea was unrealistic. We respectfully disagree. We need to find a way to enable officers and analytic staff to seek knowledge and learning. For simplicity's sake, we are calling this the '*Stanko ten minute challenge*'—that is, ask officers and crime analysts to find 10 min in any day to think, read, skim new research findings and consider evidence-based solutions to emerging problems. This could come in many guises, but we would advocate the use of something akin to our research guide and other exercises we have previously discussed and for officers to use such instruments over time to generate

[1] In UK policing, this is a knowledge-sharing portal, only available to police personnel.

E.A. Stanko, P. Dawson, *Police Use of Research Evidence*,
SpringerBriefs in Criminology, DOI 10.1007/978-3-319-20648-6_17

new research. To bring added benefit to such a direction, wider policing organisations[2] could nominate key gaps in knowledge, national risk registers, emerging threats or wish lists of research that need more attention that could be the shared topic for a collective '10-minute' thinking exercise. In this way officer and analyst research could be directed to those areas of strategic or other priority demand.

What we are saying here is that the whole approach to transformation of any policing organisation to becoming more evidence-based generators and evidence users has got to be more creative. We do need to be more ambitious. We certainly know that we might be able to persuade people to consider the Stanko 10 min per week! We too experience mush brains after a full day of reactive activity—but we have to start somewhere.

[2] In the UK this would be the College of Policing, Police and Crime Commissioners or other government agencies such as the Home Office or the Ministry of Justice.

Technical Ability of More than Police Officers

This final aspect, and again one that we feel has been overlooked previously, is the awareness that evidence-based policing goes beyond that of only police officers. Specifically, here we highlight civilian staff such as performance and intelligence analyst (or comparable) functions that many police services have. These are disciplines that in our experience are not under the professional umbrella of social research and are perceived as being separate to evidence based policing. We would argue they should not be. Our work in this area demonstrated to us that many performance/intelligence analysts are not comfortable within social research methodologies. Equally, not all (police) researchers see performance as something they ought to do. This is unfortunate as police services are a goldmine of data that should be routinely mined in more creative/innovative ways generating learning to benefit decision-making. The argument we propose, and the one we have done so throughout the chapter, is to move us away from the craving of achieving only 'gold standard' evidence—which of course can play an important role, but cannot routinely answer and arm officers within their daily work. Translating good research into the performance expectations of officers is a skill, and analysts can certainly merge best practice knowledge into crime analysis products.

Within our Evidence and Insight unit we sought to develop comprehensive problem profiles of key issues—bringing together performance analysts and researchers—pushing for creativity outside the churning of basic numbers. As an illustration, our aspiration was to lock together *performance* and *research* functions so to create an inquisitive and virtual feedback loop that supports continuous learning based upon better interrogation of data. Essentially—to turn a performance culture into a learning culture. There are two dominant examples of this fusing of professions. Both will be briefly touched upon here.

First—when we were asked to produce a rich problem profile for the 2012 Lord Victor Adebowale Independent Commission into Policing and Mental Health (Grossmith et al. 2012). There have been many calls for the police to improve their understanding and treatment of people with mental health issues (see Flanagan 2008;

E.A. Stanko, P. Dawson, *Police Use of Research Evidence*,
SpringerBriefs in Criminology, DOI 10.1007/978-3-319-20648-6_18

Bradley 2009). The Independent commission largely arose out of the latest of such calls for action in the UK; the death of Sean Rigg in Police custody during 2008. Sean was a Black British musician/producer with a history of paranoid schizophrenia who died in police custody in a South London police station. The inquest into the death highlighted numerous failings—such as the use of unnecessary police force during restraint.

To support the work of the commission, Evidence and Insight produced a wide-ranging analysis of MPS data systems to develop a holistic problem profile of mental health and the police. Our starting point on this project was to bring together learning from innovative mining of police performance data (e.g. around topics including demand, calls, victims, offenders, taser use, custody, places of safety) and original social research techniques (e.g. literature review, original surveys). The subsequent assessment considered all aspects of the end-to-end journey through the organisation in terms of police interaction. Key results included:

- In terms of journey—results demonstrated a heavy and rising demand—on average 165 calls per day involving mental health with clear borough variation. Other notable results indicated that out of the total of 231 taser deployments between September 2011 and August 2012, just over a third were linked to mental health in some way.
- Places of safety (POS)—the use of custody as a POS was seen, once again with borough variation, but overall only in a minority of cases (e.g. in 3 years only 0.02 % ($n=258$) of all detainments).
- Training—survey findings echoed previous studies and continued to indicate inadequate officer training around identification, needs and management of mental health.
- Partnership working—drawing upon our London surveys of Offender Management and other staff surveys, gaps were observed in terms of appropriate access to mental health partners.
- Audit and review—our ability to scrutinise data sources was hindered due to a lack of rigorous data collection and capture. Indeed—we encountered paper forms that were being used to document important information.

Our reflections in the final report were that felt we were only scratching the surface of understanding between mental health and the police and that the quality of captured data was not empowering easy insights. This latter point is important—without full understanding of the problem at hand—the ability to bring about successful change will be limited. This is a topic in dire need of a developing evidence base and with it meaningful improvement.

There was also wider learning for us in terms of bringing together performance analysts and researchers and how to help both disciplines work effectively together. This fusing together was an essential ingredient—but it was not necessarily a comfortable fit and reminded us of the different skill sets in play.

Secondly, when asked to develop research on 'Mobile ID', a new technology which enabled police officers to conduct mobile fingerprint identifications. We developed a piece that included both a sound performance framework (e.g. tracking basic equipment usage monthly) and a longitudinal online survey to track staff opinion of the technology over the course of the pilot. The research was to support the pilot and lasted for 8 months. It was not conceptualised as a gold standard piece; the desire was to generate learning around the technology, usage, what was working and the challenges.

In terms of basic usage, we saw 890 user accounts with three quarters of staff having carried out at least one mobile ID transaction. As the pilot progressed, we saw an increased uptake and use of the technology—a total of 13,500 transactions over the period. The performance aspect allowed us to track usage by borough and specific teams, which resulted in some devices over the course of the pilot being redistributed to maximise usage and demand: a practical efficiency improvement drawn from the data. The staff perception surveys captured the voices of 579 officers across our two waves. We saw very high levels of satisfaction; indeed 90 % of officers were either satisfied/very satisfied. Interestingly, satisfaction with the device improved over time and increased the more the device was used. In terms of positives, the officers told us how the technology changed their ways of working largely around time savings. The drawbacks the officers conveyed focussed on relatively minor aspects such as bulky cases, size of buttons and battery size and linkage to other data systems in the technology.

In both case studies, the combination of routine performance data *and* social research methods generated new insights beyond what would have been achieved in isolation. This raises the need to better integrate operational policing and crime/research analysis through training, communication and encouraging joint working. In a recent review of the integration of crime analysis into patrol work, Taylor, Baba and Egge (2013) plead for better analytic products. They identify a number of barriers to the effective use of crime analysis such as 'a police culture that is perceived to question the legitimacy of analytic work, a hierarchy that may take little notice of non-police staff … and a failure to support innovation'. We agree with their observations, but we cannot emphasise enough the importance of treating crime analysts as partners in the journey to better evidence-based working practices. Despite our seeming seniority in the Met, we too fought almost on a daily basis to integrate evidence into the narrative of the organisation's strategic and operational direction. The strength of uniformed policing culture is that it also excludes civilians from its inner circle. While we are not asking to be 'members' of the club, we are asking for parity in influence. It is this parity of influence—that of the credibility of scientific knowledge in a traditional craft based world (as Willis 2013 suggests) that must be addressed in debates about evidence-based policing. Better approaches to evidence-based policing should be formed on a renewed understanding of the partnership between civilian analytic staff and the uniformed officers who use the information for better service to the public.

And Finally, Over to You ....

In summary we have shared some of our 'craft-based' experience in this book in the hope that it will provide some inspiration that change is possible. We have since moved our team to the oversight body for policing in London—the Mayor's Office for Policing And Crime. Here the thirst for evidence-based thinking seems insatiable—a different experience that too has to be managed. We see a fertile ground for evidence based policing within the UK and elsewhere in 2015. We are confident that there is a growing (but slow!) receptivity amongst our former policing colleagues in London towards evidence based policing. The changing picture is no doubt complex and we worry that there is still confusion about exactly 'how' to be evidence led or which levels of evidence should be attributed most weight. But we are confident that the challenge is set—how can policing assimilate and embed a systematic approach to evidence-based policing into business as normal.

To see scientific evidence used without prejudice or distinction from professional experience is a tall aspiration. We believe the way to achieve this is through a corporate (whole) approach integrated into business as usual and strategic need as opposed to a wealth of standalone research pieces. We suggest that we see the best opportunity to embed evidence-based policing in a generation and make strides not seen previously. However, any evidence-based approach has to go beyond the starting points of methodological quality and has to incorporate the more nuanced aspects to be able to deliver EBP within a police service. We sincerely hope that our insights—drawn both from our successes and from the hurdles we have encountered—are able to practically support you towards better evidence-based working.

Good luck.

E.A. Stanko, P. Dawson, *Police Use of Research Evidence*,
SpringerBriefs in Criminology, DOI 10.1007/978-3-319-20648-6_19

References

Bacon, M. (2014). Police culture and the new policing context. In J. Brown (Ed.), *The future of policing*. London: Routledge, 103–119.
Bradford, B. (2011). Convergence, not divergence?: Trends and trajectories in public contact and confidence in the police. *British Journal of Criminology*, *51*(1), 179–200.
Bradford, B., & Jackson, J. (2010). *Trust and confidence in the police: A conceptual review.* National Police Improvement Agency Wiki. Retrieved from SSRN: http://papers.ssrn.com/sol3/papers.cfm?abstract_id=1684508.
Bradford, B., Jackson, J., & Stanko, E. A. (2009). Contact and confidence: Revisiting the impact of public encounters with the police. *Policing & Society*,*19*(1), 20–46.
Bradley, K. (2009). *The Bradley Report: Lord Bradley's review of people with mental health problems or learning disabilities in the criminal justice system*. London: Department of Health.
Braga, A., & Weisburd, D. L. (2012). *The effects of "Pulling Levers" focused deterrence strategies on crime Campbell systematic reviews*. Campbell Collaboration.
Briner, R. B., & Rousseau, D. M. (2011). Evidence-based I–O psychology: Not there yet. *Industrial and Organizational Psychology, 4*(1), 3–22.
Cabinet Office. (2012). *Test, learn, adapt: Developing public policy using randomised controlled trials*. Cabinet Office.
Cabinet Office. (2013). *Applying behavioural insights to organ donation: Preliminary results from a randomised controlled trial*. Cabinet Office.
Chan, J. (1997). *Changing police culture: Policing in a multicultural society*. Cambridge: Cambridge University Press.
Cope, N. (2004). "Intelligence led policing or policing led intelligence?" Integrating volume crime analysis into policing. *The British Journal of Criminology, 44*, 188–203.
Coulter, S. (2010). Systemic family therapy for families who have experienced trauma: A randomised controlled trial. *British Journal of Social Work, 41*(3), 502–519.
Dawson, P., & Stanko, B. (2013). Implementation, implementation, implementation: Insights from offender management evaluations. *Policing, 7*(3), 289–298.
Dawson, P., Stanko, B., Higgins, A., & Rehman, U. (2011). *An evaluation of the Diamond Initiative: Year two findings*. London: Metropolitan Police Service; London Criminal Justice Partnership.
Dawson, P., & Williams, E. (2009). Reflections from a police research unit—An inside job. *Policing, 3*(4), 373–380.
Flanagan, R. (2008). *Final report of the independent review of policing commissioned by the Home Secretary and conducted by Sir Ronnie Flanagan*. London: Home Office.
Goldstein, H. (1990). *Problem-oriented policing*. New York, NY: McGraw Hill.

E.A. Stanko, P. Dawson, *Police Use of Research Evidence*,
SpringerBriefs in Criminology, DOI 10.1007/978-3-319-20648-6

Gondolf, E. W. (2001) Limitations of Experimental Evaluation of Batterer Programs. *Trauma, Violence and Abuse, 2*(1), 79–88.
Grossmith, L., Franklin-Trespeuch, E., & Dawson, P. (2012). *Mental health & the police: Understanding demand and incident management in the Metropolitan Police Service.* Unpublished report.
Grove, L., Farrell, G., Farrington, D., & Johnson, S. (2012). *Preventing repeat victimization: A systematic review.* Stockholm: The Swedish National Council for Crime Prevention.
Guyatt, G. H., Oxman, A. D., Vist, G. E., et al. (2008). Rating quality of evidence and strength of recommendations: GRADE: An emerging consensus on rating quality of evidence and strength of recommendations. *BMJ [British Medical Journal], 336*(7650), 924.
Harper, G. & Chitty, C. (eds) (2005). The Impact of Corrections on Reoffending: A Review of 'What Works', 2nd edn. Home Office Research Study 291. London: Home Office.
Hohl, K., Bradford, B., & Stanko, E. A. (2010). Influencing trust and confidence in the metropolitan police: Results from an experiment testing the effect of leaflet-drops on public opinion. *British Journal of Criminology, 50*(3), 491–513.
Holdaway, S. (2009). *Black police associations: An analysis of race and ethnicity within constabularies.* Oxford: Oxford University Press.
Hollin, C. (2008). Evaluating offending behaviour programmes: Does only randomization glister? *Criminology & Criminal Justice, 8*(1), 89–106.
Hough, M., Jackson, J., Bradford, B., Myhill, A., & Quinton, P. (2010). Procedural justice, trust, and institutional legitimacy. *Policing, 4*(3), 203–210.
Jackson, J., & Bradford, B. (2009). Crime, policing and social order: On the expressive nature of confidence in policing. *British Journal of Sociology, 60*(3), 493–521.
Jackson, J., & Bradford, B. (2010). What is trust and confidence in the police? *Policing, 4*(3), 241–248.
Jackson, J., Bradford, B., Hohl, K., & Farrall, S. (2009). Does the fear of crime erode public confidence in policing. *Policing, 3*(1), 100–111.
Jackson, J., Bradford, B., Stanko, B., & Hohl, K. (2013). *Just authority? Trust in the police in England and Wales.* London: Routledge.
Kennedy, D. M. (2011). *Don't shoot: one man, a street fellowship, and the end of violence in inner-city America.* New York, USA: Bloomsbury Publishing.
Laycock. (2012). In support of evidence-based approaches: A response to Lum and Kennedy. *Policing, 6*, 324–326.
Loader, I., & Mulcahy, A. (2003). *Policing and the condition of England: Memory, politics and culture.* Oxford: Oxford University Press.
Loftus, B. (2009). *Policing culture in a changing world.* Oxford: Oxford University Press.
Lum, C. (2014). Policing at a crossroads. *Policing, 8*(1), 1–4.
Lum, C., Telep, C., Koper, C., & Grieco, J. (2012). Receptivity to research in policing. *Justice, Research and Policy, 14*(1), 1–35.
Miller, J., Davis, R. C., Henderson, N. J., et al. (2004). *Public opinions of the police: The influence of friends, family and news media.* New York: Vera Institute of Justice.
Neyroud, P. (2011). *Review of police leadership and training, two volumes.* London: Home Office.
Reiner, R. (1992). *The politics of the police* (2nd ed.). London: Harvester Wheatsheaf.
Reiner, R. (2010). *The politics of the police* (4th ed.). Oxford: Oxford University Press.
Rosenbaum, D. P., Schuck, A. M., Costello, S. K., Hawkins, D. F., & Ring, M. K. (2005). Attitudes toward the police: The effects of direct and vicarious experience. *Police Quarterly, 8*(3), 343–365.
Senior, P., Wong, K., Culshaw, A., et al. (2011). *Process evaluation of five integrated offender management pioneer areas.* London: Ministry of Justice.
Sherman, L. (1998). *Evidence-based policing. Ideas in American policing. Series.* Washington, DC: Police Foundation, July 1998.

Sherman, L.W., Gottfredson, D.C., MacKenzie, D.L., Eck, J., Reuter, P., & Bushway, S.D. (1997). *Preventing crime: What works, what doesn't, what's promising*. Washington, DC: Department of Justice, National Institute of Justice.

Skogan, W. G. (2006). Asymmetry in the impact of encounters with police. *Policing & Society, 16*(02), 99–126.

Stanko, B., Jackson, J., Bradford, B., & Hohl, K. (2012). A golden thread, a presence amongst uniforms, and a good deal of data: Studying public confidence in the London Metropolitan Police. *Policing and Society, 22*(3), 317–331.

Stanovich, K. E., & West, R. F. (1998). Individual differences in rational thought. *Journal of Experimental Psychology: General, 127*, 161–188.

Sunshine, J., & Tyler, T. R. (2003). The role of procedural justice and legitimacy in shaping public support for policing. *Law & Society Review, 37*(3), 513–548.

Taylor, B., Boba, R., & Egge, J. (2013). *The integration of crime analysis into patrol work: A guidebook*. Washington, DC: Office of Community Oriented Policing Services, U.S. Department of Justice.

Thaler, R. H., & Sunstein, C. R. (2008). *Nudge: Improving decisions about health, wealth and happiness*. London: Yale University Press.

Treasury, H. M. (2011). *The Magenta book. Guidance for evaluation*. London: HM Treasury.

Tyler, T. R. (1990). *Why people obey the law: Procedural justice, legitimacy, and compliance*. New Haven: Yale University Press.

Tyler, T. (Ed.). (2007). *Legitimacy and criminal justice: International perspectives*. New York: Russell Sage Foundation Press.

Tyler, T. R. (2011). *Why people cooperate: The role of social motivations*. Princeton, NJ: Princeton University Press.

Tyler, T. R., & Fagan, J. (2008). Legitimacy and cooperation: Why do people help the police fight crime in their communities. *Ohio State Journal of Criminal Law, 6*, 231.

Tyler, T. R., & Huo, Y. (2002). *Trust in the law: Encouraging public cooperation with the police and courts through*. New York, NY: Russell Sage Foundation.

Weatheritt, M. (1986). *Innovations in policing*. London: Croom Helm.

Weiss, C., & Bucuvalas, M. J. (1980). *Social science research and decision-making*. New York, NY: Columbia University Press.

Willis, J. (2013). *Improving policing: What's craft got to do with it? Ideas in American policing*. Series. Washington, DC: Police Foundation, June 2013.

Wünsch, D., & Hohl, K. (2009). Evidencing a 'good practice model' of police communication: The impact of local policing newsletters on public confidence1. *Policing, 3*(4), 331–339.

Index

E.A. Stanko, P. Dawson, *Police Use of Research Evidence*,
SpringerBriefs in Criminology, DOI 10.1007/978-3-319-20648-6

Printed by Printforce, the Netherlands